# Nobody Hitchhikes Anymore

# Nobody Hitchhikes Anymore

Ed Griffin-Nolan

Rootstock Publishing

First Printing: September 27, 2020

*Nobody Hitchhikes Anymore*
© 2020 by Ed Griffin-Nolan
All Rights Reserved.

ISBN: 978-1-57869-038-1
eBook ISBN: 978-1-57869-039-8
LCCN: 2020903183

Published by Rootstock Publishing,
an imprint of Multicultural Media, Inc.
27 Main Street, Suite 6
Montpelier, VT 05602
USA
www.rootstockpublishing.com
info@rootstockpublishing.com

Email the author at NobodyHitchHikesAnyMore@yahoo.com
for interviews and appearances

Cover and interior design by Tracey J. Hambleton

Artwork through the book by Ellen Haffar

Printed in the USA

*For Ellen,*
*where the road begins and ends.*

# Table of Contents

*Author Preface*     **i**

*Foreward*     **iii**

*Introduction*     **vii**

**Chapter One:** Packing It Up     **13**

**Chapter Two:** Day One     **23**

**Chapter Three:** What Does Your Wife Think?     **31**

**Chapter Four:** Waterloo to Buffalo     **35**

**Chapter Five:** The Heroin Highway     **45**

**Chapter Six:** Ladies' Day in Pennsylvania     **55**

**Chapter Seven:** Red-headed Woodpeckers and Hitchhiking Serial Killers     **65**

**Chapter Eight:** Jesus, Tuco, and Canned Fruit Cocktail     **75**

**Chapter Nine:** Don't Be a Dick     **87**

**Chapter Ten:** Tilting at Windmills     **99**

**Chapter Eleven:** Lightning and Snakes     **111**

**Chapter Twelve:** Nebraska Was Always Tough     **121**

**Chapter Thirteen:** Bacon Broccoli Slaw     **133**

**Chapter Fourteen:** Steamboat Waters to Dusty Craig     **149**

**Chapter Fifteen:** Leaving Salt Lake and Desert Fever     **163**

**Chapter Sixteen:** Itsy Bitsy Takes Me to the Golden Gate     **173**

*Epilogue: Earbuds and Tinted Windows*     **183**

*Acknowledgements*     **191**

# Author Preface

—*Ed Griffin-Nolan, Pompey, New York, April 15, 2020*

Before social distancing became our national religion, I planned to spend the early spring of 2020 hitchhiking on backroads south toward Key West. I was eager to travel with strangers and continue to write about the experience. Instead, I'm confined to the space I live in, avoiding strangers, quite literally, like the plague. A hitchhiking virus has hijacked all our lives.

I might be a serial killer and not even know it. Same goes for you.

The COVID-19 pandemic dramatically alters the calculus of hitchhiking as it altered how we think about grocery shopping, basketball games, attending worship or visiting taverns.

It changed everything. Asking strangers to invite me into the confined space of their car or truck, the thumb-out gesture at the core of the hitchhiking experience, would be not only unwise and unproductive. It would be dangerous and unethical.

The journey described in these pages took place before any of us knew how to spell coronavirus. For now, my latest journey is on hold. The virus has this in common with the hitchhiker—it confronts us with our response to fear and the unknown. The central insight of this book, that we are all in this together, that we're all on the road sometime, is being tested every day.

As we collectively grapple with this plague, we realize that it doesn't care about our status. Behind the wheel or riding shotgun— we're all potential hosts and potential victims.

Do we hoard? Do we share? When we look inside ourselves and our communities, what do we see? How do you and I take in and take on the challenge of the unknown?

Hopefully, together. Let's enjoy the ride. Thank you for reading.

# Foreword

—*Sean Kirst, Buffalo, New York, February 2020*

A lifetime ago, I joined a childhood buddy in hitchhiking our way toward the West Coast. This was 1979, and along the way we stopped in at some ancient breakfast joint in Nebraska. The man at the cash register looked us up and down and asked what we were doing. We told him, and he responded, in a grim voice that held no kindness:

"Famous last words. Hitchhiking cross-country."

Since you are reading this foreword more than forty years later, you know how well he did as a prophet. What sustained us were the people out there on the road, the same people this guy thought would be the end of us. They not only stopped to share their blankets and food and shelter but, more than anything else, they trusted us with stories that still live in us now, even with our then-long hair turned toward gray.

This all brings me to a far more daring hitchhiker, Ed Griffin-Nolan, a friend I met in Syracuse about twenty-five years ago. I was aware of him even earlier, certainly, when he was a sometimes fierce, always thoughtful, and notably prolific columnist for *The Syracuse New Times* —the now-vanished alternative newspaper in Syracuse—and I was still a sports columnist for *The Post-Standard*, a local daily.

Still, there is an interesting truth that many journalists understand from the back-and-forth every day in the hodgepodge of life that is a newsroom: You can read what people write in a newspaper, and understand a few components of those journalists, but you do not really know them. All you know is what they publicly advocate and believe, but not how or if they execute those beliefs.

Ed, I realized years ago, exercises his.

He sent me this manuscript a few days ago, and I sat down to read it on the couch, and I could not put it down. In this book, Ed kicks aside the chance to simply offer the nostalgic blarney of tales of hitchhiking in the 1970s. He decided to do it again, on the edge of 2020, to see what might happen and where we are.

I quickly realized, simply from the number of occasions on which Ed referenced the first time he thumbed across the nation, how the original journey triggered some kind of mysterious alchemy within him, how he saw in it both a dash of America as it is, and maybe even a hope for what it is supposed to be.

This book captures that wistfulness, sure, but also spills out warmth and humor and fraternity and loss, all of it delivered with a kind of heartbreaking backdrop that Ed will explain. In a way—spoiler here—the entire thing is a full-on assault on fear, Ed walking up to go nose-to-nose with some shadowy American terror of the unknown that has been unleashed with tragic application in this new era: Fear of the stranger, fear of the immigrant, fear of those who have less, fear they might want what we have.

Fear, beyond all else, of getting too close.

Hitchhiking, in essence, involves those with the elemental—a vehicle that moves—offering the most immediate of gifts to those who, at least in the moment, are utterly without. It is also a chance for little miracles, for connections and confessions, and as Ed unwinds each one within these chapters—as you meet the jobless and the dreamers and the nostalgic and above all else, again and again and again, the fundamentally kind—you realize that his journey, above all else, is an act of loving rebellion.

Taking your thumb to the road, even forty years ago, was an easier task, in a different America. There were far more people doing the same thing, and there was simply more cultural faith that the pilgrim with the backpack along the side of the road was not a threat. Instead, pulling over offered a potential break from the tedium of whatever task or trial brought you to the journey.

Indeed, the whole reason you stopped was not for the stranger, but for the companion, two identities now so at war in today's America.

Ed and I have been fellow travelers on different kinds of roads. Our earliest conversations were in the 1990s, when we were both young fathers with kids of roughly the same age. As a church schoolteacher, I came to know Ed's boys, Dan and Rob. They were funny, wry, observant, and intensely thoughtful, and in the way these things often go, the kids were the reason the dads started to talk.

Before too terribly long, Ed and I were running together, and that led into the occasional breakfast and cup of coffee. We ended up supporting each other at a difficult moment, when we both walked away from newspaper jobs that, in many ways, had been our medicine, a giant part of who we were, and which left us with little option except to take a hard look at ourselves.

After all of it, I really thought I knew Ed.

Certainly, I had heard dozens of stories from Ed about his life, little tales of struggle or triumph or sadness that he told quietly as we ran the big hilly circle around Onondaga Park. Certainly, we had shared accounts of our separate cross-country forays with friends in the 1970s, parallel adventures, when we each left our very different hometowns. Ed was from Staten Island, while I grew up in Dunkirk, a suffering industrial city along Lake Erie that makes a hard cameo in these chapters, and we were both deeply affected by those we met while hitchhiking.

Yet here is the gift of what you hold in your hands. Whatever I believed or assumed about Ed, I feel as if it is now peeled back—and I know him in a tremendously better way. A truer way, if you will. That happened simply because I read this book, and it would have been a loss if I'd kept going, if I'd looked straight ahead and passed it by.

Hitchhiking, I venture, made us into better people. Ed believes so much in the covenant of the road, that he insists it must be living hope, not history. That covenant, really, always comes down to this:

Given the chance, you can trust him on this ride.

# Introduction

"We're all on the road sometime."

Gray nodded, turned his cycle around, and rode off to start the workday. The offhand remark had been Gray's response when I tried to thank him. The night before, this stranger had collected me and my best friend Joe from the Oklahoma roadside and ferried us one at a time to his home, supplied us with pizza and beer, and let us camp in his backyard. Then he shuttled us back to the road in the morning.

It was the summer of 1978. I've forgotten a lot of things since then, but those words have stuck in my head since that day. "We're all on the road sometime."

Forty years later, wanting to believe that Gray's words still held some truth, I took off again to hitchhike across the United States, asking myself the question: Is *the road* still out there?

This book is my report. It includes cops and cuffs and canyons. Ramps and snakes and lightning. Rednecks. Hobos. Forest Rangers. InfoWars. Gun racks. Young mothers, an old widower. Meth heads. Pothead survivors. Moonshine. A Tex-Mex trucker fresh out of federal prison, high on Jesus.

In short, lots of stories.

The road, I found, is still out there. It's a place with possibilities and frustrations in limitless supply. The bigger question, four American decades on, is this one—

Is there still a thing on the road called *we?*

=

In the summer of 1978, my childhood friend Joe, a Staten Island boy long since transplanted to Boston, accompanied me as we successfully, eventfully, and sometimes hilariously made our way across the continent. We crossed into Canada at least once, camped in soaring mountains our Eastern eyes had only seen in pictures and, with only a single paid fare and a couple of nights paid lodging, arrived at the Golden Gate Bridge in San Francisco unharmed.

From California, we hitched to Arizona, descended and ascended the Grand Canyon on the same day (not advised), begged rides all through the desert Southwest, found friends in Oklahoma and rides through Arkansas, crossing back over the Mississippi to arrive in Memphis on the first anniversary of the death of Elvis Presley. The Memphis police were on strike; the party went on all night.

We followed the Mississippi south, then hitched through relentless August humidity until we arrived in the French Quarter of New Orleans, still in its pre-Katrina, pre-Disney glory. Our stay in New Orleans was enhanced by a kind uncle who gave us entrée to jazz clubs that two grubby college boys could never have afforded without him.

In time, we turned north, back to where our adult lives awaited. In Meridian, Mississippi, we hitched a ride with a family in their camper van all the way to Ohio, and after a night sleeping under a highway bridge and a few short hitches, landed back in New York State.

It's been forty years, and that trip still sticks with me as one of the finest educational and recreational experiences in what has turned out to be a pretty far-ranging life.

I decided to do it again.

This time around, it would be just me. Joe is in the throes of late middle-age, balancing retirement planning with college tuition for his two kids, borderline diabetes, and a new titanium hip. When I told him that I was going back out on the road, he shook his head and spent the better part of an evening trying to convince me not to do it.

Joe spoke for a lot of my friends and a significant minority in my family. My wife, somewhat suspiciously, wholeheartedly endorsed the plan.

Here's what they said: One, nobody hitchhikes anymore. Two, it's not safe. Three, things have changed too much. Or some combination of One, Two, and Three.

Here's my reply: I'm hitting the road. I'm not sure where it will take me. Destination is beside the point. I'm not worried; I never learned how to worry much.

At this point, in my early sixties, I've got nothing to prove.

I was nearly killed once by a drunk driver, when his airborne Grand Prix crash-landed on my 1972 Pinto at highway speed. I've had to stare down an armed Arkansas tomato farmer who didn't like my poking into his slaving operations, got kidnapped by a Nicaraguan contra with hollow eyes, had my house burn down, got married twice and divorced once, published one book and a thousand stories, raised three fine young people, started a business, buried two parents and, in the ultimate sadness, kissed a lifeless grandchild goodbye.

And they tell me I should be worried about someone I don't know just because he wants to give me a ride? Uncertainty is the only certain thing I can vouch for. Routine pays the bills but dulls the soul. I'll take my chances with the unknown.

The idea, the hope, is this: somewhere inside most of us, we yearn for connection. People still want to believe that we're in this together. We want to help one another get by. We battle our fears, our hearts get handcuffed by our schedules and anxieties but, unless I'm the outlier, I think that deep inside, most of us want to connect with each other.

In the past forty years, people have begun to think that things have gotten scarier, but in fact, for most people in our part of the world, our daily lives have gotten safer.

Fear has metastasized even as violent crime has gone down.

Fear of the open road has spread even as drunk driving has gone down.

Cars and roads have gotten safer. Consider vehicle safety. Seatbelts were optional, even for infants, when Joe and I took our trek. Today, cars have enough airbags, warning systems, and restraining devices to make most accidents, shy of head-on collision with a texting teen or an asteroid, survivable.

Consider communication. When my hard-working, understanding, tolerant parents dropped me and Joe at the Airmont Road entrance to the New York State Thruway in June of 1978, they could only expect to hear from us via a letter in the mailbox or a collect call. Today, I carry a computer in my pocket that's more powerful than NASA had in 1978, and my friends at Google can tell the world exactly where I am at every moment.

Today, I can upload in real time a picture of every driver I meet, or text to my family the license plate of every car I climb into. In a moment of distress, I can speed dial any one of a dozen people. This time, I expect, it is going to be so much safer. Except, as Joe kept reminding me, I'm older now and traveling alone. Yeah, whatever.

Danger is down. What's up is fear. We have become fearful beyond reason. Fear has become the cultural and political currency of our time.

Of course, I might get killed. Some beady-eyed lunatic might decide to track me down using that little Google device and do his very best to do me in. For the record, I travel unarmed—better for everyone involved. Should someone succeed in stalking me and putting an end to me, it would be sad.

No, it would really piss me off to have to concede, drawing my final breath, that my hypothesis was fatally flawed.

Turns out that was not the case. It was America—fascinating, boring, hypnotizing, and full of surprises. A changed world with a similar landscape. A nation divided by geography and race and history, united by quirkiness and suspicion and a desire to share our stories.

It was a blast. Come along.

# 1

## Packing It Up

There are two old backpacks in the attic, one green, one rust colored. The rust-colored pack is a large open sack without compartments or frame. The green one is supported by an aluminum frame, has upper and lower zipped compartments, and zipped pockets all around the sides and top. These adornments create the illusion that a backpacker can keep everything readily accessible and at hand.

I am exceptionally gifted at losing stuff. I've been known to misplace a bar of soap on my way to the shower. Looking forward to having less stuff, easy to locate and harder to lose, I decide to take the green one.

I pack a lightweight nylon hammock with a zipper to keep the bugs out and a canopy to keep the rain out. Perfect for spring and early summer camping. Just add trees.

What else?

**Water.**

At the sporting goods store, my water bottle options are limited to lightweight .75-liter size collapsible tubes or monster three-liter bladders. I prefer something in between. The day before I leave, my old friend William shows up with a gift—a 1.5-liter indestructible Nalgene bottle that fits perfectly in a side pocket of my super-efficient green backpack!

**Bugs.**

You may worry about serial killers. I worry about mosquitoes. Forty years later, I can still hear Joe's voice hollering and swearing as we flailed and danced and swatted to fend off a menacing, buzzing horde of skeeters that attacked us one late Arkansas evening. It was rice country, nothing but paddies on both sides of the road for miles and miles. We were stuck halfway between Little Rock and the Mississippi River, staring into a setting sun and swatting our own faces, trying to fight off the swarm.

An angel coincidentally also named Joe, who had come back from Vietnam with ears so damaged that he could only hear us if we shouted, stopped his four-door Plymouth sedan and plucked us from the swarm just as the buzzing and biting started to threaten our sanity. "Get in quick," he drawled. "Them mosquiters'll 'et you alive."

He wasn't kidding. Bugs won't kill you, but they'll make you wish they had.

I got myself a bag of wipes that promised to contain only natural bug repellents and stuffed them in a side compartment. Then I got a spray pump bottle with DEET, just in case the bugs hadn't read the labels on the eco-friendly wipes.

**Food.**

In 1978, before the creation of magazines and podcasts teaching people with too much money how to live simply, Joe and I were frugal out of necessity. We carried two hundred dollars each, most of it in traveler's checks. Traveler's checks, for the millennial reader, were sequentially numbered pieces of paper issued by American Express. For a small fee, they gave you a way to travel with money and recover it quickly if you were robbed or just lost them—the more likely scenario, in my case. Sort of like changing the PIN on your debit card after it goes missing.

Our scant funds meant that we cooked our own food on a Coleman stove, mooched off friends or, more often than you would think, were fed by strangers. People who gave us rides in their cars often shared their food, as well.

We carried a cook stove and a few pots. We hard-boiled eggs whenever we could find a place to boil water and slapped peanut butter on bread and called it lunch any time of the day. I'd venture that many of us today spend more in one visit to a coffee shop than we spent that summer on a week's worth of food.

We had signed up with a temporary employment agency, so we could work when we ran out of money. But we traveled so frugally with that two hundred dollars apiece, we never had to stop to work along the way. We each came home with money in our pockets. I remember, it was twenty bucks; Joe insists we each had fifty. Maybe he was holding out on me.

On this trip, most of my food will be made from plastic.

My Visa card. For moments in between restaurants, I load up a few packets of instant oatmeal, a bag of raisins, and a summer sausage. These can hold me over in a pinch. No cooking utensils. No thought of a stove. I'd rather spend a few bucks at a Denny's or a McDonald's than carry a kitchen with me.

Why spend time heating up water to make bad instant coffee? In the past forty years, an entire profession has been birthed—the barista, and I fully expect an army of them to be waiting to fulfill my caffeine needs at every highway exit.

I'm not rich, but on this trip, I won't have to watch every penny, another benefit of no longer being twenty-one.

### The Sign.

In 1978 we carried a yellow legal pad covered in plastic, and each morning we wrote the name of the town we hoped to reach by evening.

This time I have a long thin Styrofoam sign printed with a digital destination. It reads #NobodyHitchhikesAnymore. I plan to hold it up to the passing cars with one hand while I raise the other thumb to the sky.

**Footwear.**

One pair of boots and a pair of sandals. When I'm not hiking or standing roadside with the pack, I'll switch out into the sandals. They also will double as water shoes. My Oboz boots have made it through multiple hikes in the Adirondacks, the Rockies, and one long foray through the Chobe National Forest in Botswana, without giving me so much as a blister.

I'm taking along six pairs of socks, the most comfortable socks I can find. The package says that they do not smell. I believe that they do not smell while they are in the package, but when I put the sock on my foot and my foot in my boot, after stewing a few days, they will test the limits of truth in advertising.

The hardest decision was whether to take my running shoes. It should be a matter of space and convenience, though a simple choice this is not. I've run and coached runners for two decades. Running is a part of who I am. I just don't know if I can fit the shoes into the pack, or if it will be worth hauling them around for the few opportunities I might have to squeeze in a run.

When you slim the volume of your possessions, you decide to leave parts of yourself behind. You uncomplicate your life, but you find that the choices you make will add new levels of complication. Running shoes are tied to my friends, my kids, my dogs, to all the places I've run, from the Finger Lakes to the streets of Managua, to a volcano on the island of Java.

I am not a fast runner, but I can run anywhere, and forever. It wasn't always so. In my twenties and thirties, I smoked heavily, Marlboro Reds, up to three packs a day.

My advice to people who want to be old runners is not to be young runners. While friends are all breaking down, replacing parts and getting treatment for miscellaneous ailments, I seem to stride on with hardly an ache or pain. Smoke heavily through your twenties and thirties, I kid them, then start running at age forty with the meniscus of a teenager.

About ten years ago, after half a dozen marathons, I started coaching distance runners. My friend Brendan talked me into it. Six marathons later, and I started to get itchy to qualify for the Boston Marathon. Regular marathon runners like myself, not the elite skinny African guys you see winning New York or Boston or the Olympic marathons, silently sort themselves into categories.

There are the Finishers. Anyone who can knock out 26.2 miles has done something to be proud of. Then there's Sub-Four. If you can do a marathon in less than four hours, you are taken more seriously. And then there's the BQ. Boston Qualifiers. It's a badge of honor.

Why would any sane person want to wear that badge? Probably for the same reason that someone might want to hitch across the USA. Sanity is not part of the equation.

The Boston Marathon is the Super Bowl of our sport. To run Boston, you must qualify by running another marathon at a pretty good clip. The qualifying times vary by age group and are set by some oracle in the Bay State, most likely a Red Sox fan.

In my early fifties, the oracle said that I had to run a 3:45 race. That's 26.2 miles in three hours and forty-five minutes, about eight and a half minutes per mile. I could keep that pace for about eighteen miles, and then something would always go wrong. In five races over the course of two years, I fell short by two minutes, three minutes, and once, after an awful series of calf cramps, by almost fifteen minutes.

Brendan was a masterful coach. He knew everything there was to know about human physiology, and even more about the psyche of runners. He had a story to tell for every situation you might face in training or in a race. Slender and balding, he had the cutest smile and a wry sense of humor. He was a reader, well versed in any topic that came up on our long runs.

Brendan agreed to coach me one-on-one, with the goal of getting to Boston. I was a compliant athlete eager to please my coach. Early morning runs, core workouts, interval training—we did it all, until finally, in January 2011, I broke 3:45 in the Charleston Marathon. The oracle of Boston opened the gate and, along with twenty thousand other fit people lacking in common sense, I ran from Hopkinton, Massachusetts, to Commonwealth Avenue in Boston, 26.2 miles in broiling heat, in April 2012.

Five years later, Brendan and I were both competing in a relay race in the Finger Lakes. It was a pretty spring day. I was waiting for my team near the top of a hill. Brendan was on a different team.

I saw him coming up the hill. I cheered for him. He waved.

Then he fell.

And that was it. All the efforts of all the paramedics couldn't save him. A friend and I each held one of his hands. We told him we loved him. Maybe that helped his spirit. It did not restart his heart.

I still can't put together in my head that I watched a dear friend, and the healthiest athlete I knew, fall down in front of me and never get up. But that's part of what I take with me when I think of packing those running shoes.

This life of getting up and going to work, of going out to run, of hugging the people you love as you say goodbye, these days and nights of pleasure and pain and knowing and seeking, of getting through a day's work to collapse in another night of sleep—they don't go on forever.

I leave the Mizunos under my bed and hope to run in them again when I get back home.

### The Place I Leave Behind.

I live in an old cobbler shop built, we have learned, to make boots for soldiers heading south to fight in the Civil War. It sits right smack in the middle of New York State, close to Syracuse, near a green little town called Pompey. Our home sits on a creek. My wife and I fixed it up twenty years ago. Between her gardens and artwork, my roofing and woodworking skills, and a lot of determined love, we made it a place of great memories for our three kids and their multiple dogs and cats, rodents and fish, and the occasional reptile.

It's a peaceful refuge from "the city." New York City family and friends laugh when I call Syracuse "the city." In the five boroughs, that is a term reserved for Manhattan.

But Syracuse is my city now. It is a prideful town straddling the old and the new economies. It's a city that struggles with abandonment. We've been abandoned by half our people, by most of our industry, and that shakes the hardworking hopeful attitudes that built a place like this. There are parts of Syracuse that inspire a sadness you won't find in Managua or Mexico City, a shabbiness in some neighborhoods that feels shameful for its proximity to revamped places with names that end in Hill or Square.

We cautiously hope this new economy that has come creeping our way will bear fruit for those left behind by the old, but there is a crusty fear that it will pass us by. We watch new buildings rise, resumes get polished, careers take off, and tax incentives doled out without much noticeable result. Unlike our downstate friends, our town, with its fifteen hundred vacant homes, can't afford not to get excited when an Amazon beckons.

Statistics tell us that Syracuse is the thirteenth poorest city in the United States of America. People think New York State is just Manhattan, a few farms, and Niagara Falls, but Upstate contains six mid-sized industrial cities strung together by the Thruway, each of them teetering, in varying degrees, on the brink of collapse ever since I got here forty years ago.

We welcome immigrants while still confining generations of African Americans to the worst schools and neighborhoods. Syracuse University, best known for its basketball and lacrosse teams, hosts a large center for veterans and military families, as well as a vibrant resistance culture. Students last year shut down the campus after a series of racially motivated threats.

Syracuse has a big heart that defies snowstorms and trend lines. We continue to hope.

I first set foot in Syracuse on that cross-country trip with my friend Joe, in 1978. My first real job interview took place on East Genesee Street, as I wandered, clueless, through a manufacturing town that was wandering cluelessly toward the end of industry. Syracuse launched me on a decade spent in labor and human rights struggles across Latin America, and then it drew me back with its seductive blend of community, cross country skiing, and cheap housing.

Sometimes when I think of leaving Syracuse, which I doubt I will ever do, I think that it might be nice to live in a place where you don't have to work so hard, constantly pushing the boulder uphill. In some sense, Central New York is America. Most of the people in the city are black and brown—the surrounding towns and suburbs are whiter and wealthier. The city votes reliably Democratic, the rest of the county goes with the Republicans.

But our Congressional district has flipped between parties five times in the last six elections, making us either the biggest flip-floppers or the most open-minded people in the nation. Syracuse last year put an independent in City Hall after decades of Democratic dominance. Donald Trump won upstate, while Hillary Clinton, who visited here regularly as a US Senator, took not only New York City but urban Upstate areas as well.

I love my city, with all its challenges, and I love this staggeringly beautiful and sometimes shabby piece of the country. In no small way, the hope that I have for America, and for this hitchhiking journey, comes from living in this community and knowing people who care deeply and welcome newcomers with open arms. I'm counting on finding a lot of rides from people whose hearts might be in the same place as my neighbors', even if their politics reside somewhere to the right of mine. Admittedly, there's a lot of room there. I'm counting on the categories meaning less as the miles add on.

Syracuse, my family, and my friends, like the running shoes, are all part of a great life that I am leaving behind. With all its stories and hopes and failures, it is a big part of what I take with me.

# 2

## Day One

It starts with a rain delay. The skies over Pompey open up, and it doesn't seem to make much sense to go out there and get drenched. I wait around the house, unpacking and repacking, playing with Gracie, our energetic four-year-old lab-poodle mix, and checking weather reports. Listening to thunder. In short, procrastinating. I am excited for this trip. Been thinking about it for years, but when the moment arrives to step out the door, I waver.

Maybe it's true.

Maybe nobody hitchhikes anymore.

And maybe they have good reasons. Maybe they are smarter than me.

My house is warm and familiar. I love my wife. When she comes home after school, we could take the dog for a walk at the park. She might even make me dinner.

Whose idea was this, to head out into the unknown?

At around eleven, there is a break in the clouds, and I finally saddle up the backpack.

Immediately, I notice that this pack seems much heavier than the one I hauled forty years ago. In 1978, it weighed forty pounds—this time it is just under thirty, but it feels like a ton. My legs and arms are strong, but I wonder how my shoulders are going to hold up. I waddle down the brick path to the gate, swing it open, shut it behind me, and I'm on my way.

The backpack straps cut into my chest. Already this seems like a very bad idea. I turn right onto Watervale Road and start walking. Uphill. There is nothing but hills between me and the road west, Route 20, the old Cherry Valley Turnpike.

Within minutes, my breathing gets heavy. This older version of me has a few advantages over the kid from 1978. For one thing, I don't smoke any more. Second, I've learned how to listen to my body and to pace myself. The years have given me respect for what can happen if you don't. There'll be no Grand Canyon heroics on this trip.

Halfway to Route 20, I take my first break, a stop outside my friend Ralph's house.

There is some debate among hitchhikers as to whether you are more likely to get a ride if you're moving and hence demonstrating effort, commendable by most peoples' lights, or if it works better to stop and station yourself facing traffic, which allows drivers to get a good look at you and have a chance to make eye contact. In my case this break isn't a choice—I have to get this damned pack off my shoulders.

I set the frame against Ralph's mailbox, rest for a few minutes, and indulge myself by entertaining the possibility that Ralph might be home, take pity on me, and give me a ride up the road.

No such luck. After ten minutes, I load back up and set off again, leaning into the hill, holding a steady three-mile-per-hour pace. The sun is peeking from behind the clouds. Magnolia and dogwood trees bloom on the roadside. Milk tanker trucks climb along the ridge of Pompey Center Road, a mile to the east. Peeper frogs hop into the creek as I approach.

They, too, must have gotten the memo that hitchhikers are to be feared. Cars that pass me on Watervale are driven by friendly, older people in nice cars, going about their day. These are my neighbors, and while most of them wave, none of them stop. Not a good sign.

In little less than an hour, I arrive at the intersection of Route 20. I lean my backpack against the Stop signpost at the corner, at the base of a steep climb to Pompey Hill. A plumber, an appliance repair crew, a bakery truck, all pass by headed east. Fog starts to drop down the hill from the west.

And then, all of a sudden, there's Rob. My first ride. He pulls his brand-new Toyota Tacoma over and tells me to toss my pack in the pickup bed. He explains that he's only going a mile up the road. The truck is so clean and new, I apologize for my wet boots. He says not to worry. Rob tells the story of a brother who hitchhiked to California in the '70s. Rob had always admired him for that. He offers to take me a few miles further, to the stoplight at the Pompey Mall, a local gas station owned by our friends, the Neugebauers, people with a sense of humor about their station in life.

Everyone in Pompey knows the Pompey Mall. Before we get there, we figure out that Rob's wife is a massage therapist, like me, so in a way we kinda know one another. Not surprising in this small town.

That first ride turned out to be a window into what was to come. Many of the people who picked me up had three things in common with Rob: They drove pickup trucks, they knew someone with a hitchhiking story, and they went out of their way to drive me to a place where I would have a better chance of getting a lift.

Kim doesn't drive a pickup, just a small SUV. It is just starting to rain when she pulls up and opens her door. I am just across the street from the mall, at the intersection of Routes 20 and 91, at one of the highest points in Onondaga County.

Kim is a retired art teacher. My wife also teaches art. It's starting to seem as if our tribes are looking out for me already. Kim tells me how she loved hitching when she was younger. In 1980, she and her boyfriend hitched cross-country just after graduating college.

Women like Kim are clearly in the minority among hitchhikers, and among rides. But there are more women who pick up guys thumbing than you might imagine. In 1978, we had a decent number of solo female drivers and even more families that included moms who thought nothing of letting us into their kid-laden vehicles. And we would see women hitching rides, rarely alone, usually, like Kim had gone, accompanied by a man.

Kim is a sweetheart. In her retirement, she goes back to city schools in the afternoons to teach art in after-school programs. Life is good, she says, and she drops me in Lafayette, offering a hug with her goodbye. I cross over Interstate 81 and climb another hill, pass a McDonald's and climb the hill to a Byrne Dairy gas station and convenience store, slipping into a booth just as another deluge hits.

Byrne Dairy has a sandwich counter that makes a pretty good tuna melt. The cashier, a young lady named Sahara, randomly asks me if I have anything special going on today. I tell her that I hope so, and she is happy to take one of my wristbands.

The wristband is the brainchild of my running partners, Michelle and Willson. The week before I set out, they presented me with a box filled with hundreds of green and yellow speckled rubber wristbands. On the outside, they'd stamped the website where my blog is housed—*NobodyHitchhikesAnymore.com*—and on the inside a simple, Thank You. Each time I hand one out, I feel thankful for such good friends and hopeful that I'm meeting a new one. Sahara is very cool.

Sitting at the booth, eating my sandwich, I charge my phone and strike up a conversation with a pair of school bus drivers and with Patricia, the local school secretary. Patricia leaves, wearing a

NobodyHitchhikesAnymore wristband, and a minute later she runs back in to tell me that there is a man in a car with California plates filling up at the gas pumps!

He takes off before I have a chance to see if he might be my ride. I go back to my sandwich, thinking that it would have spoiled the fun, anyway, to ride all the way to the Pacific with just one driver. (I did get a two-day ride across Argentina, back in 1979, but that was during a railroad strike—long story.) If getting to California had been my only goal, I could have just taken the bus. Or taken up an offer from my friend Dave, a long-distance trucker.

When Dave first heard of my plan, he was panicked, fearful of what would befall me out on the road. He told me to wait and he would find a load going west and take me along. I declined his kind offer. Dave survived years in Vietnam and a lifetime on the open road, but even he was worried that some form of evil would find me out there, hitchhiking.

Two minutes after I get back out on Route 20 West, a nice late-model mini-SUV stops and backs up toward me. Marc opens his door and says Hi. Turns out we kinda know one another from meetings around Syracuse. Marc is a web marketing guy.

Marc gives me a ride up Route 20 to the intersection of Route 80, where he turns off toward home. He asks to borrow my phone. Right there on the side of the road, Marc sets up an Instagram account: @NobodyHitchHikesAnymore. And just like that, I am on two social media platforms, exactly two more than existed in 1978.

He drops me near Beak & Skiff, an apple orchard that has reinvented itself as a brewery, a distillery, and a concert venue. You find a lot of that in post-industrial New York, where ingenious people find ways to get a buzz or make an event out of a grape or an apple or even a humble potato. Beak & Skiff grows everything you need to make vodka or bourbon, and their self-pick apple orchards go on for miles. It's as American as apple pie.

Twenty minutes after Marc the web guru leaves me, a sheriff's patrol car pulls up, lights flashing. As much as I try to look innocent, taking in the clouds, looking up and down and all around, it soon becomes apparent that I am the inspiration for the officer's visit. The deputy sheriff is very polite and informs me that he got a call about a suspicious person walking along the road asking for rides. He asks for my driver's license and while he is running my credentials through his dashboard computer, a second deputy pulls up behind him.

The sheriffs in Onondaga County drive massive Ford Explorers that make Humvees look puny. And there are the lights, the noise, and the passing cars. We are becoming a spectacle. Now I'm the guy on the side of the road by the distillery and the apple orchard with the two patrol cars, jellybean lights flashing, radios squawking, and homebound commuters rubbernecking. The deputies and I have become entertainment for the late afternoon commute, and I'm wondering how this is all going to play out.

The first deputy gives me back my license and confirms that his dashboard computer can find no trace of criminal activity on my record. He informs me that it is against the law to hitchhike in New York, which, further research later reveals, is not entirely accurate. He asks what I'm planning to do, which is a relief, in that it implies that I am still at liberty to pursue my own happiness and not about to be given a ride to jail, which might mess up an already rainy first day.

I tell the two law enforcement professionals that I once hitchhiked across the country in my reckless youth and that I am now doing it again. The first deputy had not yet been born in 1978, but the second cop, the woman, his superior officer, was a kindergartner at the time. They both shake their heads and warn me that times have changed, and hitchhiking is not only illegal but dangerous.

They ask if I am armed, sounding for all the world like they are hoping I will nod in the affirmative. They seem deeply concerned. I tell them I have done this all over the world, but they remain very certain that this world has changed. The junior officer insists, "There are a lot of crazy people out there."

"They'll shoot you," says his boss.

Wow. She didn't say they *might* shoot me; she says they *will* shoot me. Just wow.

How many times have I been told about how bad the times have gotten and how dangerous this world has become? Those fearful opinions drip from screens and bellow across the airwaves, but they usually emanate from politicians, commentators, or barstool patrons who can't be taken as serious sources. They usually have no basis for knowing. But these two uniformed officers are in a position to know.

I reported for our local weekly paper for fourteen years, so in this moment, before these two law enforcement officials, my journalistic antennae start to rise. I recognize that this is a unique moment—I now have the attention of two valuable sources, people who can tell me from their own experience about the grave dangers of hitching rides.

If you were one of the people driving by on Route 20 West that day, you were probably thinking that I was some loser about to get arrested. In fact, I was prepping for an interview.

I ask each of the deputies if they know any cases of hitchhikers being harmed. Neither of them can recall one. I ask if they had personally attended to any cases in which a hitchhiker had harmed a driver. Same answer. Negative.

These two folks have a combined quarter-century of service in uniform, and what stands out is the difference between their attitudes and their actual experiences. The junior officer insists that the danger is real, even though he hasn't met any of the victims or perpetrators. He offers that the paucity of casualties is because, "Nobody Hitch Hikes Anymore." That's what he says, word for word. Not wanting to be mistaken for a wise guy, I glance down at my sign and say nothing.

Clearly, these cops do not want to arrest this gray-bearded pilgrim. Nor do they want to spend the remainder of the afternoon fielding calls from frightened soccer moms. Their immediate concern is that they will soon get another call about this suspicious person and then have to return to the scene of the crime and do something about him.

They do not want my stubbornness and the public's panic to force them to violate their better judgment. They obviously do not wish to apprehend the perpetrator, i.e. me, and take me into downtown Syracuse to the strangely labeled "Justice Center," which reasonable people just call "the jail." Arresting people for nuisance crimes or victimless crimes is a time-consuming bother for police. Good cops much prefer negotiated solutions, so they can move on to more important matters. If the public will let them.

"Look," says the younger officer, "you can't stand on the side of the road with your thumb out."

I press him a little. "Not at all?"

He squints. He sighs. He takes off his hat. He shifts his weight from right to left, looks up at the sky, then down at the ground. He looks me in the eye and rephrases his request. "You can't stand on the side of the road with your thumb out—in front of a police car!"

It appears that we have come to an understanding. The deputies climb back into their thrumming Explorers, shut down the whirling light show, and proceed west. I exhale.

As they drive over the hill and out of sight, I initiate a new routine, based on the advice of the sheriff's deputy. As cars come toward me, I look both ways for any police vehicles before holding up my sign and putting out my thumb.

Five minutes later, Rich pulls up and I am on my way to Skaneateles. Rich kindly drives me through the charming lakeside village and deposits me on the western edge of town. There I stand for an hour and a half, watching residents—mostly fearful soccer moms—leave town, while wondering if they plan to turn me in to the cops. I keep walking and, before dusk, I cross the line into Cayuga County.

Now I am a different sheriff's headache.

# 3

## What Does Your Wife Think?

The terrain shifts quickly, just west of Skaneateles. I walk about a half mile to a gas station, where I purchase a cup of coffee, even though I don't need it.

This is my idea of fair trade. I buy a cup of coffee or a chocolate milk in exchange for use of your restroom and maybe a few cents-worth of electricity to charge my phone. In this case, the deal also includes your bench to sit on while I think through my plan for the night. It is already past six.

On the way to the coffee pot, I notice a sales display advertising Confederate flag decals. It always confuses me when Northerners celebrate their rebellious side by brandishing the banner of the losers of the Civil War. This display is a clear sign of how quickly the politics and social norms change in this part of the state, where cities tend toward the blue and rural areas go red, though for the life of me I don't see how red bleeds into Confederate stripes.

After a half hour of people-watching, I saddle up and head west. Route 20 skirts the northern edge of the Finger Lakes, a series of beautiful glacier-made lakes ideal for boating, fishing, and sailing. Skaneateles is one of the smaller lakes, but thanks to the Clintons and other famous visitors, it has made a name for itself as a freshwater version of Martha's Vineyard. The rest of the Finger Lakes Region wobbles on the edge of revival and decline.

I walk past idyllic lakeside vineyards and shuttered auto dealerships, fields full of rusty farm equipment, and some high-end spas and resorts. Just up the road, someone has plastered an "Impeach Cuomo" bumper sticker on a lamp post.

The political divide between neighbors upstate usually has a lot to do with guns. Andrew Cuomo, New York State's governor, passed a gun control measure in 2013, called the SAFE Act, just after the school shooting in Newtown, Connecticut. He's been hated by a large swath of rural and suburban Upstaters ever since.

That doesn't keep the city folk from electing him again and again, but outside the cities, the SAFE Act stirs rebel souls. A ten-minute ride or two hours walking could get me to the city of Auburn, located at the northern tip of Owasco Lake. If you visit Auburn, be sure to see the home of Harriet Tubman, the nineteenth century freedom fighter.

Absent a felony conviction, you won't be allowed into the town's other attraction—the state prison, site of the world's first execution by electric chair. Fifteen miles and one lake west of Auburn, is the town of Seneca Falls, famous for its groundbreaking 1848 conference on the rights of women, and reportedly the inspiration for the hamlet of Bedford Falls, from Jimmy Stewart's holiday film, *It's a Wonderful Life*.

So, there is a lot of history on this highway, but for the moment I'm not getting any closer to it. Cars buzz by me. Nobody even slows down.

A woman in an SUV flashes me the finger. Really? I wonder if she was among the concerned citizens who called the cops on me earlier in the day. That's a kind of nasty I just can't understand. If you don't want to pick me up, fine. You've got the car, I've got nothing but my boots, and in mere seconds I'll be in your rearview mirror. Why flip me the bird? I do not return the salute.

In an optimistic moment earlier in the day, I had hopes for making it as far as Buffalo. At this point, a ride to Geneva, 35 miles west, would be most welcome. I am getting hungry. That tuna melt and a Baby Ruth bar from the Pompey Mall are all I've eaten since breakfast. I have walked a total of nearly six miles.

With each step toward the setting sun, I scan the roadside for a place suitable for hanging a hammock. I think about my comfortable home, about my dear wife, about dinner. I wonder what Ellen is making for dinner. Probably something better than a gas station burrito.

There is a question everyone asks when they hear I'm going hitchhiking. "What does your wife think of this?" There is an alternate phrasing, usually posed directly to Ellen, "How can you let him do this?" Her answer: "Do you think I could stop him?" She lets her head go back in a big laugh.

And then there are those people who ask straight up if my wife thinks I am crazy, to which we both reply, "Yes, but this has been known for quite some time."

I've been talking about this trip forever. Any time Joe comes to visit, the topic of the summer of '78 comes up. It is of far greater significance to our life stories than the place we grew up, the games we played, or where we went to college. Even after a lifetime of travel, we still refer to that hitching adventure as "The trip."

Her response to this present adventure was classic Ellen. "Fine with me, just don't ask me to come along."

People expect her to be worried, but she doesn't go there. She thinks it more likely that I'll spend stretches of time bored and possibly sunburned. The axe-murder scenario doesn't keep her up at night. I did make sure that she knows how to find the folder with the life insurance policy. This morning, before she left for work, I asked how far she thought I would make it on the first day.

Seneca Falls, she replied, suggesting that she had given this some thought. She kissed me goodbye and offered to come get me if I got stuck. The offer had a geographic limit—anywhere this side of Seneca Falls. She wasn't sure I'd make it that far. That's Ellen in a nutshell— kinder than she lets on, and she knows her limits.

As the mosquitoes of Eastern Cayuga County begin to make their presence felt, the idea of seeing her appeals to me much more than spending the night at the edge of a muddy bog. I make the call. She says she'll come get me. But I'm not going back home. Just get me to Geneva, I ask.

Geneva's ten miles west of Seneca Falls, but she's true to her word, and she loves me. Ellen packs up Gracie the wonder dog and rides off into the evening. I stand at the roadside with my thumb out as she pulls over. In part to soothe my pride from this momentary admission of failure, I pretend that we are strangers as I get in. The dog does not buy into the subterfuge. Gracie assaults me with the enthusiasm only an overgrown puppy greeting a member of the pack can muster.

As we drive west, I replay the day, filling Ellen in on the ups and downs and the maybes of the journey so far. Will there be more cops in the morning? How many days will it take to get across the country at this pace? I have covered barely fifty miles of a very large continent.

You can't really let math get in your head if you're hitching. There is no such thing as a typical day. That's what I keep telling myself. If I tried to extrapolate from this day's rides, I would be lucky to make it to South Dakota in time for Christmas.

Ellen takes me to the Quality Inn of Waterloo, further west than her Seneca Falls, but not all the way to my Geneva. I thank her and kiss her goodbye while Gracie wags and wiggles in the backseat. The dog, like most of the beings who know me, is confused. What is happening?

Ellen has to be at work early the next day. So do I.

# 4

## Waterloo to Buffalo

I prefer back roads. That explains why the pace of my travels is
only a tad speedier than a diligent bicyclist. You get shorter rides
on Route 20 than you would on the Thruway, but the terrain is
more appealing and the likelihood of drawing the attention of law
enforcement diminishes.

The New York State Thruway, officially named for Governor
Thomas E. Dewey, a man who was, for one moment in November 1948,
known as the next President of the United States, is just shy of five
hundred miles long. It runs from just north of the New York City line
to the Pennsylvania border, most of it laid in the 1950s. It was renamed
for the former governor, who had firmly opposed funding it.

Dewey was still alive when the legislature voted to name the

Thruway after him in 1964, violating one of my few non-fungible political beliefs, that politicians who want stuff named after themselves should first be in their graves. The toll charged for a car to cross the entire state in 1978 was less than you pay today just to cross the George Washington Bridge.

After stuffing myself with pancakes, tolerable scrambled eggs, and some fruit salad at the Quality Inn, I position myself on the side of Route 20 West. My spot is just before a turnoff to NY-414. If someone is going west, they could take me on 20, but a ride north on 414 to the Thruway remains an option. It is a good spot, near a Tops Market, which means that someone who wants to pick me up but can't stop in time would be able to pull into the parking lot and holler to me.

Sure enough, a truck pulls into the parking lot, and a guy comes running over, hollering. I ask him where he is going. He has the same question for me. Steve fixes refrigeration units for the grocery store chain. He is reporting for work, but he wants to let me know that he saw me at the edge of Skaneateles last night. He loved my sign. It says, #NobodyHitchhikesAnymore. He promises to pick me up if I am still waiting here when he finishes work. I give him a wristband, we shake hands, and part in mutual admiration.

Steve helps restore my faith in Skaneateles, battered a bit by the police intervention, the Confederate flags, and the nasty driver blithely flipping me the bird.

It isn't long until another Steve stops his GMC mini-SUV and offers to take me to Geneva. This Steve is seventy years old, a mustachioed barrel of a man. He grew up in the Finger Lakes area, and he has the easy, unhurried way of someone happily retired. He was one of sixteen children and, as a young adult, he and a friend loved to ride motorcycles all over the Eastern US and Canada. He grins and tells me stories of sleeping in farmers' fields, and of dropping quarters in a metal box to turn on the water for a warm shower at a roadside rest stop in Maine.

Steve is a homebody these days, reveling in the joys of being a grandpa. He has a secret yearning that he shares with me. One day, he hopes to convince his wife to take a cross-country ramble with him. When the road gets under your skin, it becomes a persistent condition.

Looking out the passenger window, I notice that we passed Lowe's Home Improvement, where Steve is headed. He drives a good five miles past his destination to get me to a better spot. We shake hands, and off I go.

The air outside Geneva is sweet. I lean my pack against a pole, pull out my notepad, and sit leaning on the pack, taking notes. There's a Walmart in the strip mall behind me. The lovely little lake town of Geneva, like a lot of places, has traded in a bit of its identity for survival. I can see a Dollar Tree, a few used car dealerships, and a Salvation Army Thrift Store on the main road through town.

Suddenly, my throat wants to close. I feel choked by an overwhelming odor of dead animal. Then there's that fresh-air sweet smell again. I keep jotting things down, and the stench returns, the olfactory equivalent of fog, making me gag.

That's when I remembered reading about The Dump.

The Seneca Landfill in Romulus is not far away, and trucks hauling trash in, or coming back out empty, are blowing by me on the road, creating this fleeting nauseating effect. Seems like it would be tough to live near such a nasty dump. I grew up on Staten Island, within a bike ride   of the World's Largest Landfill, where the other four boroughs of the world's greatest metropolis dumped their trash daily. So, I feel you, Romulus and Geneva.

These trucks are headed back to Western Pennsylvania and as far as Ohio to gobble up more trash to dump in this pristine part of the Finger Lakes.

Reading up about the Seneca Landfill in Romulus, I discover two things that have changed in the past forty years. One, even garbage dumps get reviews on Google, and two, PR agents (excuse me, digital branding specialists) shamelessly endeavor to spin shit into gold. The Seneca Landfill's homepage leads with the cheery headline, "Keeping Western Pennsylvania Clean." For balance, I would substitute something like, "Making Hitchhikers Wonder What Died Here." Another reason I never went into PR.

Suddenly, Dave.

Thank God, because if I sit on the side of that road long enough, not only do my clothes start to stink, but I can come up with more absurd thoughts than I can scribble, and I can learn more by listening to voices not emanating from inside my own skull.

The back of Dave's red Chevy pickup is filled with an orderly collection of a working man's tools. He has done all sorts of construction work in his life, and at age sixty-one he has settled into surveying.

Our ride together lasts about fifteen miles. Dave and I have a lot to discuss. He sailed for years on Cayuga and Seneca Lakes. I tell him about my sailboat, the Carol Ann, an eighteen- footer named for my late mother. He loves cross-country skiing. We get talking about our favorite places to ski. Dave and I sense right away that we are of the same tribe. Sailboat guys tend to cross-country ski. Motorboat guys like snowmobiles.

I ask about what goes through his mind when he sees a hitchhiker. A driver only has a few seconds to decide. To pick me up, Dave had brought his truck to a halt on a two-lane highway and made not one, but two U-turns.

He asks if I've had any problems with law enforcement.

I tell him about my meeting with the sheriff's deputies back near Beak & Skiff.

His reply is honest. "You're not black, that makes a difference."

I've heard these same words before. In March, my son Robert and I had spent a day hitchhiking along Colorado's Eastern Range. Dale, the driver of a battered Caravan, left us off thirty miles from Boulder with these words: "You'll be fine here. You're white. That helps."

Dave tells me about a hitchhiker he picked up on this same road through the Finger Lakes a few years back. It was getting near dark when he saw the man on the road headed east from Canandaigua to

Geneva. The guy was black, he was deaf, and could speak very little. He pulled out a notepad and scrawled on it in pencil.

"I'm a veteran."

The man indicated that he had been hassled by the police in a town where he clearly looked different from almost everyone else. He'd hid his backpack in the woods in a futile attempt to blend in. Dave took him back to get the bag, then drove him to a McDonald's that was on his route. The man didn't have money for food, so Dave gave him five dollars. He doesn't know what happened to him.

In that story, I could feel Dave's yearning for kindness. And I sensed that we shared a frustration with the limits of individual kindness in the face of evil.

There is an intense communion that can occur between two strangers who have taken a risk and chosen to be in one another's company. People tell you things. You tell them things. I'm not with Dave long, but in our brief visit I tell him about Caroline.

Caroline is a little girl I never met who wakes me up every day with a question. She's my granddaughter, born and died on the same day in December 2017. I don't know what her question is. It comes to me in a dream state, and I don't usually remember my dreams. And I never hear her voice. Never see her eyes open. Stillborn is an unfathomable word. How can you be dead before you're born?

Caroline was some kind of miracle. My son Daniel, her father, had inherited a family tendency toward marinating our brains in alcohol. Caroline's mother, Jules, lived with her own demons. The pair had met right at the crossroads of hell and a new life. My beautiful boy and his new-found love were on the edge of recovery, a moment when things could go either way, when they learned that a baby was expected.

And everything changed.

We learned that she was a girl. Dan and Jules named her Caroline. Then they found out that Caroline had an extra chromosome, the trait that causes Down Syndrome. They pushed on.

She's going to need a lot more love, Dan said.

The two expectant parents moved into the house where I had raised Dan and his brother decades ago. A burst of love followed them. Friends appeared with paintbrushes, pizzas, hammers, and mop buckets, filling that house with all the love that a child could ever want. Cousins visited. An uncle gave them his used car. Ellen, Dan's stepmom, threw a baby shower that was just precious. It was beautiful to watch. It was all good.

The kids and their fellow drunks and addicts and friends scrubbed and polished and worked all day, went to their meetings at night. In two weeks, the place was transformed. Christmas was coming. Jules blossomed. You never saw a pregnant woman work so hard. She was radiant, in love with her child and the new life that she and Dan were building. The house filled up with presents. They had two weeks to go, and I was feeling like a lucky man.

When your son comes home to tell you that he knocked up the girl he met in the halfway house, you really don't know what to expect. We were fortunate beyond belief. Our beautiful boy had met a beautiful girl. They set up the nursery in the same room where I had assembled Daniel's crib, a lifetime ago. It was a house Dan loved, where he held memories of childhood, a house he had once painted and often repaired. Now he was working and dreaming of making more memories for a child of his own.

The moment I learned that Caroline was coming, something inside me knew that I could never make this hitchhiking trip. I wouldn't want to be away from her. I couldn't imagine not holding that baby girl.

I still can't. I still can't imagine how this life can go on without holding that baby girl.

But now she is going with me. I'm taking her on this trip. I can leave town because I know my son and our new daughter, Jules, are both healthy and safe and, in their agonizing grief and persistent recovery, they have all that love their Caroline inspired to comfort them and get them through whatever each day or hour brings.

I'm proud of them. I'll miss the three of them more than anything.

But they're coming with me too.

It's the first time I've said all of this, and Dave, a stranger in a red Chevy truck, listens. We talk about loss and hope and the things that keep us going—and our realization, as two men chugging through their sixties, that one day, things will stop.

Dave must have sensed I was hungry for tales of kindness.

It is a comfortable truck. I realize that I can barely breathe. Kindness fills the air, stronger than the stench of any landfill.

As we come into Canandaigua, we start to figure out the best place for Dave to drop me off, switching our conversation back to logistics in the way men do to avoid too much intimacy. I mention that I am also hungry for food.

And there it is—Wegman's. The true religion of Central New York. The mecca of grocery lovers. Our familiar, giant, local chain that sells everything. Dave makes another U-turn and gets me right to the door of the Wegman's Market Cafe, where we say our goodbyes. Thanks, Dave. Sail on.

Wegman's grocery stores are big. The layout is open enough that a guy with a backpack can walk in without drawing obvious attention. They serve warm meals and have a seating area with ample space for me to lay my pack down and go to the buffet. You best be careful at the Wegman's buffet, because it all looks good, but you don't want to fill that plate too much. It's not the all-you-can-eat kind of buffet. Here you pay by the ounce.

I load some green beans and meatballs and salad onto a plate and butter a couple of rolls, stuffing them in my pockets. When I finish my plate, I take advantage of their restrooms to wash my face and brush my teeth. In the mirror, I see men shuffling in and out, trying not to look too long at the guy with the backpack and the hiking boots, brushing his teeth in the grocery store men's room.

On the way out, I stop for a cup of coffee. The lady behind the counter, Kelly, asks me what I'm doing. "Hitching across the country,"

I say, and I tell her about our 1978 trip and what I'm hoping to do this time.

Kelly has a pleasant face and a no-nonsense demeanor. "My dad used to hitch all the time," she volunteers. "He was an alcoholic and had so many DWIs. My mom left and he raised us by himself. He was a mason and worked in Rochester. He got up and hitched to work every day. He worked hard every day."

I ask how her father is doing. My late father was also an alcoholic who went to work every day. Kelly's dad, she tells me, is sixty-four now. He can barely walk. She helps care for him.

All this transpires in the minute-or-less that it takes to pay for a cup of coffee. I hand Kelly a wristband. She slides it on her wrist, and we say goodbye, two children of hard-working drinkers, shaking hands and giving one another a look that says we probably have a lot more we could talk about.

These chance meetings with Dave and Kelly feel like meeting parts of myself, a feeling that would come back to me again and again as I make my way up the road.

I cross over Route 20 and a few minutes later, a handsome, slender guy in a Panama hat and a blue Oxford shirt comes running toward me, waving with one hand and pointing with the other hand at his ancient Honda Odyssey minivan idling by the side of the road. I hustle the pack onto my back and run as best I can. The pack is still more work than I can handle without some heavy breathing.

I throw it in the back and climb in the front. There are two empty children's car seats behind me. Rogo says he's got a few sales calls to make. He's got a lot going on. He lived in Colorado for years, ran a company for a while, and when that went under he came back to Rochester, his hometown, with his wife and two little ones. They set up their work schedules so that one of them can always be home with the kids.

Rogo says he's a vegan. Buddhist, too. He roamed a lot as a young man, subsidized by a trust fund from his father. Then his stepmother changed the will. Hence the 2002 Odyssey and the move back east, where you can buy a house for the cost of a down payment on a condo in Boulder. But he seems happy and philosophical, holding forth freely on topics ranging from the importance of fathers in the development of a child's language skills and the feelings he's gone through as each of his parents passed on. Then he asks the question.

"You got grandkids?"

Oh, Lord. It must be the white hair. I tell him a bit about Caroline. Not much. I'm not ready for that again, not so soon.

Rogo is rambling. I'm not sure he has a legitimate plan for the afternoon. We do make a few stops at auto dealerships. His mind seems fixed on his kids, a three-year-old and a five-year-old. I find it endearing, the way he can't stop talking about them. He was just going a few miles up the road. Then he offers to take me further, to the Thruway. We keep talking, and before long he changes his mind and says he'll drive me all the way to Rochester, an hour and a half west.

I text an old friend in Buffalo, which is nearer. My friend is free for dinner. Rogo drops me at the Greyhound station—a bus is leaving for Buffalo in 20 minutes. And then this thing happens. As I get out of the van, Rogo thanks *me*. Rogo shakes my hand and thanks *me* repeatedly.

I protest. I should be the one thanking him, but there is no denying that he is grateful to have found me there on the side of the road in Canandaigua. As I am grateful for him.

I wait for the bus, taking advantage of an outlet by the window to charge my phone. Green uniformed Immigration and Customs Enforcement agents check papers of selected passengers getting off the westbound bus. Everyone who gets off, gets back on.

I follow, take a seat, and reach for my phone. I panic when I realize that it is still inside the terminal! The driver lets me out and I run in to find the phone, still charging, on a windowsill. I didn't have to worry about such things forty years back. I sit back down relieved, the door hisses closed, and I am on my way to Buffalo.

# 5

## The Heroin Highway

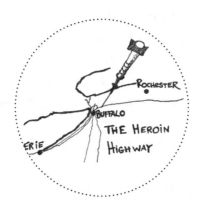

The guy who picks me up in Buffalo is a paragon of staying put. Sean Kirst is our greatest regional writer, a lover of all things Upstate New York, a man who can say, with convincing honesty, that his once-orphaned parents, who grew up in the height of Buffalo's industrial boom, thought of themselves as living in Imperial Rome. Sean parachuted out of what used to be our hometown paper, *The Syracuse Post Standard*, as it shrank and twisted and digitized like so many others. He tells the stories of upstate better than anyone else, and he holds out a dogged hope for the revival of these former Erie Canal towns currently stitched together by the Thruway. He is also a great friend.

We eat dinner at a Mexican restaurant and walk around downtown while Sean points to wisps of hope, bits of evidence to buttress his belief that upstate is ready once again to flourish. We visit his perch in the newsroom of *The Buffalo News*, the paper smart enough to take Sean and his talents in. It is a cavernous room in an enormous building. The telephones are straight out of the 1980s. The desks appear to have been donated from the principal's office of a downsizing Catholic school.

I meet his colleagues. We all know that this kind of print operation is living in hospice care, but if you've ever worked at a newspaper you can't help but love the smells and the sounds of news being collected, written, printed, and delivered.

Sean has his own stories of hitchhiking. He and his friend Paul took a trip in the summer of 1979, not unlike the journey Joe and I made. They combined bus rides with thumbing all the way across the West. He remembers the return home to Dunkirk, New York, a town of sixteen thousand souls that had already begun to bleed people and industry, as a life-changing event; he's never been able to see his hometown or state with the same eyes. His hitching buddy, Paul, still lives in Buffalo.

Back at Sean's apartment, we chatter like two kids at summer camp, swapping stories and memories until it is time for me to curl up on the floor and get some sleep.

The next morning, May 17, Sean treats me to breakfast, then drives me along the Buffalo Skyway over the Buffalo River, before leaving me about a dozen miles south at a spot along Route 5 near Hamburg. He has been checking with friends and they seem to think that this is a good place to catch a ride.

The Buffalo skyline sits off to the east, and giant power-generating windmills poke out of the mist on the edge of Lake Erie. It's a vision we never saw in 1978.

Route 5 runs between the Thruway and the fourth-largest Great Lake. My spot is at the entrance to a park with a fitness center, so people are coming and going for most of the hour and a half I spend there.

One man stops to ask, politely, "How far are you going, sir?"

I tell him I'm hoping to make it to California, I have three weeks, and I'm trying to replicate a trip I made forty years ago. He offers to take me a mile up the road.

I ask if that would be a better spot than this one.

"You got a pretty good spot here, sir."

I thank him, and he says goodbye, adding, "Good luck, sir."

I used to be called "son." Now, I'm "sir." That's what forty years and a gray beard will do.

At the side of the road, I think about the people driving by and try to figure out a posture that will invite them to stop but also communicate to them that I don't blame them at all for getting on with their day and passing me by. As each car passes, I open my thumb hand and give a little wave, turn and smile at them. It's my way of saying it's all good. I only wish that more of them would wave back.

A sheriff's van goes by and takes no notice of me. A Hamburg police car cruises past and then stops a speeder within sight of where I stand. The cop writes a ticket, then backs into a parking lot and sets up his next speed trap. Clearly, he has better things to do than worry about a hitchhiker.

A young man in a bright blue Oxford shirt stops. John looks like he's coming from a job interview, which he is. John is hoping he can get this job, which pays fifteen to seventeen dollars an hour, a big bump from the ten-fifty he earns now. John would rather be working as a blacksmith. That's his hobby, and he explains how he cooks his own charcoal and forges iron with it.

"I like keeping the dying arts alive," he says, a comment that could just as easily apply to hitchhiking. But neither hobby pays the bills, and there aren't many jobs around here that do. John leaves me near the town he calls Derby, but which is now becoming a weekend getaway destination for those who can afford a second home. People are starting to call it by a name that sounds like a resort but doesn't sound like home to John—Highland on the Lake. The town he knew is going south quickly.

I never asked where John was applying for work, but Derby is known for producing the baseball caps worn by Major League players. The New Era Cap Company guarantees Major League Baseball that every cap worn by their players is made in the USA. Derby is the last northern plant to make them. Hundreds labored there making good wages, up to twenty dollars an hour, if their hands were swift. Townspeople took pride in watching their handiwork appear on ESPN when the games were telecast. New Era is such a big presence in the Buffalo area, the stadium where the Bills play football is named New Era Stadium.

I thank John for the ride. He tells me that just before his dad died, he told John to do good whenever he got a chance. I ask him his dad's name. "James," he says.

James raised a good man. I hope John gets that job. And I hope it isn't at New Era. Just before Christmas, the company announced that they were moving production of their baseball caps to Florida. The Derby plant closed in June, 2019.

John drops me at a gas station where I am overjoyed to find a large stash of Wild Cherry Life Savers—my favorite—and I purchase a new supply of sunscreen. I'm afraid I left my original tube back at my friend Sean's. In the gas station bathroom, I manage to spray sunscreen in my eyes, only to find there are no paper towels. After splashing lots of water on my face, probably rinsing off half the sunscreen, I push on.

There's a school close to the nearest intersection, and rather than arouse the suspicion of the principal, I decide to post myself a bit farther west. I make my way to a stoplight. A beat-up blue pickup blows by and turns into the parking lot of the Tops Supermarket. A voice hollers out, "Where you going?"

It's Portia. Portia is on her way home from her job at Denny's. She's looking to take a nap at the house on the edge of the Seneca reservation, where she lives with her dad.

Portia is pretty and petite. She's got on a pink top, jean shorts, and sneakers with pink laces. The truck is a mess; both the cab and the bed are strewn with scrap lumber and auto parts. The truck lurches and roars, and Portia, smiling like the happiest woman in the world, cigarette in her lips, shifts the gears of her truck and starts telling me her story.

She says she stopped because she loved my sign. But it's more than that. Portia had to hitchhike once to Texas, to save herself from a bad situation. She was thirteen years old. She made it safely, to be with family. Life moved on, and when she came back to Western New York, she joined the legion of men and women in this part of the state who got hooked on heroin. Four years ago, she realized that the only way she could get clean was to leave, so she hopped a bus and white-knuckle-detoxed as she rode toward Colorado, where her mother lived.

Today she is celebrating four years of recovery and loving her new life.

Portia takes me along Route 5, following the flat course of the Cattaraugus Creek, leaving me in the parking lot of the McDonald's in Silver Creek, just past Thruway Exit 58. She insists I take her picture with the sign she loved so much. #NobodyHitchhikesAnymore. We hug. "I love you," says Portia as she gets back in the truck.

We had been together for less than half an hour. There is power in that connection, when you've both been on the road, and when you both have experience with demons. Out on the road, you get a lot of blank stares, but you get a lot of hugs, too.

Waiting for my Big Mac (God, I love those things as much as I should hate them) I hear a middle-aged couple talking about going to their son's graduation in Ohio. I approach, congratulate them, then inquire about the possibility of a ride west. They have clearly been together a long time, as the man didn't even have to look in his wife's eyes to know what she was thinking.

"I'm sorry," he answers, tossing his burger trash into the can and heading for the door. I smile and shake his hand as he apologizes again. There is no reason for him to apologize—I might have done the same if I were on my own, or had my wife been along.

On a few occasions, I have picked up hitchhikers with my kids in the car. Usually it was on Route 30, a ribbon of road that winds through the Adirondack Mountains. Up there, young people working summer jobs don't have cars and rely on campers to get them from work to home and back again. Usually my wife and I oblige, and they are grateful. Nobody gets hurt and it is no big deal.

Over by the Thruway ramp, I make out the silhouette of a woman standing next to a suitcase, holding out her hand. Back in 1978, it was common, if you found a good spot, to have multiple groups of people hitching. We all understood how it worked. Those who arrived last went further up the ramp, and the first ride that stopped went to the person or group first in line. You didn't cut ahead of anyone. We had a code.

That hasn't been a problem so far this trip. Cindi is the first fellow traveling hitchhiker I meet. After she tells me her name, she keeps talking, rambling really. There isn't another phrase I can understand. I try speaking to her, and what comes back to me is unintelligible. I hear something about family in Pennsylvania and some disconnected Bible verses. Cindi is sunburned. She slumps. She looks like it has been days since she has slept indoors. Abruptly, she turns and wheels her suitcase across the ramp, back onto Route 20, heading east under a bridge.

It still makes me sad when I think of her.

Cindi has barely disappeared from sight when a State Trooper pulls up. Officer RJ Smith got a call from someone concerned about Cindi. Not finding her, he seems content to chat with me. He suggests that I move a bit farther away from the entrance ramp. Hitchhiking, he reminds me, is illegal anywhere in New York State, but on Thruway property the prohibition is actually enforced. He runs my license, we chat a bit, and I pass on what little I can about Cindi's state of mind.

"You're obviously not an ax murderer," chuckles the officer as he hands me back my ID. I cross Route 20, thinking to myself—Obvious to whom?—remembering Dave's experience with the black veteran. Would things have gone as smoothly for me, were I a black man? Things cross your mind on the road.

I'm not walking for long when an ancient, red Ford pickup pulls over and stops a hundred yards ahead. When someone pulls over, you can never be sure if they are stopping for you or for some other reason. I still have my backpack strapped on, so I pick up the pace and make my way toward the truck, hoping it will not pull away.

The slider window opens. A boot drops out from the cab into the bed of the truck. Then another boot. This is followed by a raincoat, some trash bags, a good number of aluminum cans and assorted other junk. I take this as a good sign. Whoever is driving this pickup is clearing room for me in the front seat.

I get in and thank the man, who says he can get me to Dunkirk, where he lives. Carl has a long wiry beard, sunglasses, and a head of hair covered by a blue denim baseball cap. He is stone cold silent for at least the first ten minutes. This truck has no seat belts. The dashboard rattles to an extent that I fear it might shake itself loose.

A radar speed detector sounds a fake alarm every few seconds. Carl navigates in and out of little towns along Lake Erie in this noisiest of vehicles as if it were just another day. Pretty soon I notice that we are passing through Dunkirk.

Carl slowly opens up. He is on his way back from the Seneca Reservation. He went there to purchase cigarettes at $2.20 a pack and gas for the truck. In the seat between us sits a motorcycle battery to replace the one that died on him this morning. He doesn't like driving this truck, but today he has no choice, since the motorcycle, a Honda 950, wouldn't start. My good fortune, I realize, is a result of his hard luck.

He tells his story of moving from town to town, following his wife's military family, and trying to find work to support his four-year-old daughter, Shiloh. Shiloh lives in Florida now. The marriage is ending, and he won't get to see his little girl until August. He's been through a lot in just twenty-eight years on Earth. He looks like he could be forty.

Coming from a small town with dwindling possibilities, Carl has tried everything from joining the Air Force to backbreaking farm labor to long-haul trucking. On one haul through West Virginia, he fell asleep at the wheel, wrecked the rig, but walked away unscathed. At least physically. Now, every time he's in a truck, it's hard. Flashbacks, trauma come home.

Hence the preference for the motorcycle.

Carl has lived all over the country, but for now he's back in Dunkirk working as a machinist. The plant where he works, unlike New Era and most of the factories in the area, has deep local roots going back a century and a quarter. Carl doesn't think they're going anywhere.

Once Carl gets talking, his stories seize hold of him. In between the sounds of slamming gears, rattling fenders, and the beeping of the cop detector, his sorry stories of how alcoholism and drug use have eaten up his family and friends, fill the jostling cab.

As we blow through Dunkirk, he tells me of an uncle who took heroin mixed with the opioid carfentanyl. That uncle is buried in a cemetery just across the road from the park where he had injected that drug, for the last time as it happened, into his neck. Carl's mom is on Oxycodone for life, ever since her shoulder surgery.

He asks if I mind if he smokes. How polite—it's his truck and the windows are open. He lights up, then announces that he's driving me all the way across the state line, to the town called North East, Pennsylvania.

If North Carolina's back roads can be called Tobacco Road, Route 5 in Western New York should be named Heroin Highway. Nearly everyone I met along that strip that divides the Lake Erie vacation homes from the Appalachian-like towns and hamlets just to its south, seems to have been touched in one way or another by addiction.

The industrial belt that began to rust just as Joe and I were hitching through it in the late '70s, became the Rust Belt of the late twentieth century and is now the Opioid Belt of the early twenty-first.

Heroin is still killing people in Erie and Chautauqua Counties, though the numbers of fatal overdoses has started to dip, thanks to widespread use of Narcan, the drug that can bring you back from the edge of death if administered in time.

Not everyone is so lucky. Carl's uncle was one of the people who had overdosed in a park in Dunkirk a year ago. On that one weekend, eight people in Erie County alone died of heroin or fentanyl overdoses. In some cases, the toxicology reports showed both. Without Narcan, the northern stretch along the lake from Buffalo to Erie would be a graveyard. Medical examiners talk about hundreds of dead. Cops talk about thousands who would have died if someone didn't get there on time.

As it stands, there are stretches filled with the walking dead, addicts who can be maintained but remain untreated. And guys like Carl are struggling to make it, to keep ahead of the bills and the sounds of things all around him, things falling apart. Carl drops me in the town square of North East.

I walk toward the interstate and pop into a gas station for something to drink. A bearded, tough-looking guy sees my pack and asks where I'm going. He offers to take me the six blocks to the highway entrance ramp. There is a Quality Inn there, and I thank him.

His name is Jim. He's waiting in line at the register and he tells me to put my pack in the back of his truck. "I'll be right out."

I walk out toward the gas pumps. The sticker on the back of Jim's truck reads, "No one ever burned a flag at a gun show." Probably accurate, I think to myself, and I climb up into the seat to wait for Jim.

In six blocks, I didn't expect we would have much time to talk about guns and such. I am just grateful for the ride. But there is that intimacy that being in a confined space for a finite period of time can bring on. Jim and I just met and are together for less than ten minutes. What he chooses to tell me, unsolicited, during that short ride, is that he had quit drinking thirty-three years ago, when his first child was born.

Good for you, Jim. I think I just ran into a friend of Bill W., who founded AA.

Food options at the Quality Inn are limited. I walk into the bar and order a pizza and a Sam Adams lager, planning to take both the food and the beer to my room, type up some notes, watch the news, call my wife, and fall asleep. Waiting for my pizza, I overhear two men and two women, white people, chatting loudly. They are making plans for a bonfire.

"Jack couldn't get a Confederate flag, 'coz they don't let you buy them online. So he got a Trump flag for the bonfire."

Wow, I wonder what else is burning at that bonfire.

"But you can get ISIS flags," the other guy kvetches, in a talk-radio aggrieved tone of voice.

The conversation, in a room of all-white people, goes on at high volume. They seem very concerned that the movement to remove Confederate statues from prominent public places would soon be at their Pennsylvania doorstep. "Now they're coming after George Washington and Lincoln."

It is not clear to me why these folks think that black people—the obvious "they" in this sentence—would be trying to erase the memory of the president who defeated the Confederacy and signed the Emancipation Proclamation, but remember, this is a bar, and we are all white people here.

"But they want to keep Martin Luther King! He gets a national holiday."

Oh, Lord. I keep my calm, collect my pizza, order a couple more bottles of Sam Adams, and retreat to my room.

#NobodyArguesInMotelBarsAnymore.

# 6

## Ladies' Day in Pennsylvania

I wonder what kind of day awaits me as I step out of the Quality Inn, tucked up against the onramp of I-80 westbound on a sunny Friday morning. I'm not one to let a gun show bumper sticker or a beer drinking posse in a motel bar, fantasizing about getting Confederate flags to fly at their bonfire, intimidate me. But I must admit that the characters who introduced me to North East, Pennsylvania, last night did leave me a bit uneasy.

I set up on the ramp, my belly full of pancakes and coffee and my pockets stuffed with an orange and a banana from the breakfast buffet. The ramp is narrow and short, not an ideal spot.

That hardly matters. Before I even drop my pack, Gordon and Andrew Post pull their red Ford Excursion to the shoulder and invite me to hop in. Gordon runs a vegetable farm and an apple orchard, relying heavily, he tells me, on Mexican workers, since there is no one else around here willing to do farm labor. He and his family are Methodists, devoted to their church's mission in Cuba, where Gordon says he travels all the time.

This morning, he and Andrew are out getting tools for their farm, which largely functions as a CSA, which means Community Supported Agriculture. You pre-pay for a share of the produce, sparing the farmer the burden and risk of taking out high-interest loans. In return, you get whatever the fields are producing each week. The CSA had yet to be invented when Joe and I hit the road in 1978.

Gordon and I cover a lot of ground in ten minutes, but then he turns off, dropping me at Bay Front Road in the heart of Erie, Pennsylvania. In our short visit, I learn Gordon has never picked up a hitchhiker before; and neither he nor Andrew have ever hitched.

I thank them both and walk to a gas station for a cup of coffee. Having filled up on the complimentary breakfast at the Quality Inn, where I consumed calories enough for both breakfast and lunch, I don't require yet another cup of coffee. Except I imagine that I might be standing by the road here for a bit, and no longer being a smoker and having no one to talk to, I need something to do with my mouth. This makes about as much sense as this whole endeavor.

My phone rings just as I get back to the entrance ramp. It is a reporter from Syracuse, an acquaintance of mine by the name of Marnie. The hometown crowd is eager for a report on how their lonely pilgrim is faring in the wilds of Pennsylvania.

Marnie's first question also contains an answer. "Well, who picks you up? I mean, I wouldn't pick you up!"

I laugh, and before I can reply, another red SUV halts, and the passenger door swings open. Inside, four cheerful children, all belted in car seats, are wiggling their arms like gummy worms and bursting with excitement to tell this stranger that they are on their way to the zoo. Their energetic mother, Lydia, waves me in.

I sit in the front seat, pivoting toward the rear to listen to all four—Jackson, Lindsey, Lily, and I'll be damned if I can recall the littlest girl's name—tell me how they had just dropped lunch off to Dad at work and now they are going to see the lions and the elephants.

Then I remember that Marnie is still on the phone. She is stupefied that a young mother with children has picked me up. I promise to call her back in a bit.

The zoo in Erie is home to six critically endangered species, including a Golden Lion Tamarin from Brazil and a Visayan Warty Pig from the Philippines. If there is a taxonomy of cuteness in the animal kingdom, these two creatures should be about as far apart as a hummingbird is from a buzzard. You know it's a special kind of big-hearted town that will fund its zoo to help save a Filipino pig with warts—exactly the kind of town where farmers and mothers with four kids in the car will stop to pick up a hitchhiker.

The kids are most interested in seeing the tigers—and getting French fries at Arby's. It is going to be a very special day for them. I'm dropped off before tigers and fries and wave goodbye to them, feeling certain that this day could not possibly get any better for me.

Then it does.

Morgan is next. She drives by slowly and keeps going. Ten minutes later, she returns. She had seen my sign with the hashtag and looked me up online. Not sure what to do, she phoned her husband Eric and asked if it was okay to pick me up. He said sure—just be safe.

Morgan is driving an aged Buick Lucerne, which was the high end of the Buick line after the company stopped making the fabled LeSabre. Morgan has two kids, including Harmony, a seven-year-old girl with heart and thyroid issues. Next week, she's taking her to the Children's Hospital in Pittsburgh.

I had to ask why a mother with two little ones, not to mention four dogs and plenty on her mind, took the time and trouble to come back through town to give me a lift. Is this just a social media thing? Maybe she wants to be part of something that is starting to get some traction on Instagram and Facebook? I hope not.

Not the case at all. Morgan is one of the tribe. At the age of fifteen, half her lifetime ago, she had to get out of Texas. Her father had fallen back into serious drug abuse, and she couldn't take it any longer. All she wanted to do was get to Pennsylvania to be with her grandmother.

Not wanting to worry Grandma or spend money on a bus ticket, Morgan hit the road, hitching north. Two kinds of people picked her up—families and truckers. The families wanted to keep her safe. The truckers? Turns out they were friends of her Dad. Even in the depths of his battle with addiction, he put the word out to his friends on the road. They watched out for his little girl when he could not.

She thumbed all the way from Texas to Erie without letting her grandma know she was coming. On the way, a lady named Lisa, from Wheeling, West Virginia, stopped with three kids in the car. She gave Morgan a ride to a Walmart, where she had to do some shopping. "You can wait outside the car, or you can come in with us," Lisa told Morgan.

Roadside stops force hitchhikers and their rides into a delicate dance. Even though some degree of trust has been acknowledged by the very act of riding in the same car, you both know that your bond is based more on hope and faith, a cosmic collision, than on verified experience. Like any new relationship, it is untested and fragile. Whether you're stopping for food or gas, or just to use the bathroom at a rest area, you don't want to let the other person out of your sight.

It's awkwardly tricky if one of you has to use the bathroom and the other does not. If you get out and take your bags with you, you are making it obvious that you don't fully trust your companion. If you leave your stuff in the car, hoping for the best, it's going to be an anxious, possibly unfulfilling potty visit.

Your mind plays tricks, dancing between hope and conniving, when you are all alone out there on the road. On that West Virginia day, fifteen-year-old Morgan made a snap judgment and told Lisa she would wait by the car. She could keep an eye on her bags and make sure no one came along and drove the car away.

Lisa locked the car and took the kids, daisy chained hand-in-hand, across the parking lot and disappeared into the retail monster. Morgan walked around the lot, always keeping the vehicle in her line of sight. It was about a half hour, which felt three times as long, before the mom and the kids returned, dragging a bunch of plastic bags.

"Here, honey." Lisa handed Morgan a bag of stuff—a pair of sneakers, a sweatshirt, T-shirt, and two pairs of jeans. She had sized Morgan up the way only a mother can and bought her clothes to replace the skimpy things Morgan was wearing. "Honey, it's cold up there in Erie! You can't go to Pennsylvania wearing your Texas clothes!"

Our worst fears, I learn again and again, usually turn out to be nothing more than fears. Mother Lisa probably had her own story of a kindness that she was paying forward, and now Morgan was paying that kindness forward by picking me up.

Then she goes above and beyond. Morgan decides, like Rogo and Steve and Carl before her, and like so many others I would meet later, to take me beyond her destination. She is just going a few miles west of Erie, but we are having such a great time, she floors that Buick and pushes on westward.

A few minutes into our ride my wife calls, and Ellen has a chance to thank Morgan for picking me up. I hear the excitement in Ellen's voice. Was it the thrill of knowing that my hopes were being fulfilled, or relief at knowing she would not have to drive into the night to retrieve me?

Morgan is funny and tough, and God, she is happy. So happy!

Morgan loves Erie. As Rust Belt cities go, it's a lot like Syracuse, except that Erie is losing people and industry at a greater clip. Syracuse has gradually stabilized its population at around, while people are still leaving Erie. New people come in from all over the world, but not enough to make up for the exodus of locals, most of them headed south looking for work. Morgan, who grew up in the country, loves the city and its new arrivals. "Erie has a Little Italy, a little Chinatown, and lots of refugees. I like that."

It had never occurred to me, but hitchhikers and people of the road are probably more likely to welcome others who've come from far away. We tend to be curious about others. We may speak different languages, but we hail from the same tribe.

About seven and a half percent of Erie's population was born outside the US; in Syracuse the comparable number is twelve and a half. That may be one reason why Syracuse is starting to kick its lethargy and is growing again. The population of Erie recently dipped below one hundred thousand.

A woman like Morgan, with a sick child, has better things to worry about than being overrun by immigrants. Morgan leaves me at a truck stop with a vaguely erotic sounding name—Love's Plaza in Conneaut, Ohio. Love's is a truck stop chain that I would get to know well in the coming weeks.

Morgan had driven me a little over thirty miles. We take a picture together; I buy her a soda, on this side of the state line officially called "pop," and we hug goodbye. I ask her to keep me posted on how Harmony's hospital visit goes. She promises.

It is a perfect afternoon for hitchhiking. The sky is clouded over; the temperature sits in the low seventies. I am on the ramp to westbound I-90, leaving Conneaut. A car comes rolling along, driven by a middle-aged man in a short-sleeved shirt. In the passenger seat is a woman in a sweatshirt. I wave in my usual friendly way and then, to my astonishment, the little black SUV stops.

Mike gets out. "I know you!" he calls out.

Mike looks as strait-laced a character as you would expect to see driving past you on the Interstate, except he didn't go on by me. He stopped. Wait, did he say, "I know you?" Because I don't think I know him, or I didn't before now.

Then his wife gets out. "Well, I don't *know* you," Mike begins, "but I saw you back there, at the Wegman's in Canandaigua. You were brushing your teeth in the men's room."

Well, I'll be damned. Yet another one of the many benefits of proper oral hygiene. I remembered being dropped off at the Wegman's by Dave the kind surveyor, and the exchange with Kelly at the coffee counter about hardworking alcoholic dads, but I can't say that any one face in the restroom at the grocery store stuck in my mind during that brief stop.

I am very glad that Mike remembered me. He and Nancy are delightful people, among the lucky Central New Yorkers to have both of their adult children living nearby. They make the trip from the Finger Lakes to Eastern Ohio at least once a month, though they fear this might be their last time. Mike's ninety-three-year-old mother is in hospice care there.

Neither of them has ever hitchhiked, but they get a kick out of telling me about some retired friends who traveled Route 20 cross-country in a 1973 MG.

Before I embarked on this trip, I asked friends what question they would like to be asked by a hitchhiker they might pick up. The most memorable reply was this: "Avoid the dreadful 'What do you do?'"

I have followed that advice, with the result that I cannot tell you what Mike and Nancy do for a living. Like most of my rides, they had more pressing matters to talk about.

In our forty-five minutes together, we share thoughts and feelings on what it is like to say goodbye to those who brought us into the world. One thing I tell Mike is that, when a parent dies, we become a child again. Don't forget that, I advise. And I remind Mike to give himself credit for doing what he has been able to do for his mother, because there is always so much more that you want to do.

As we approach Willoughby Heights, the home of the Cleveland Clinic Family Health Center, Mike begins to figure out which exit on the Interstate offers me the best prospect for a ride south. My plan is to head toward Peninsula, where my good friends, Pat and Karin, the ones who sold me the tent I left behind, have lived for twenty years on the edge of the Cuyahoga Valley National Park.

Anyone who knows just a little bit about Ohio knows the word Cuyahoga. It's the name of the river famous for catching fire, inspiring the passage of the Clean Water Act, the creation of the Environmental Protection Agency, and the brewing of the award-winning craft beverage, Burning River Pale Ale.

That fine ale is brewed in Cleveland by the Great Lakes Brewing Company, using Lake Erie water. Forty years ago, even I had enough sense not to drink beer brewed with Lake Erie water. Now it's on the hipster list of Cleveland treats not to be missed.

While any creature with olfactory glands knew there was a need to clean up the sludge-filled waters rolling into Lake Erie and elsewhere in the industrial heartland, the outrage that bubbled up in the aftermath of the 1969 fire on the Cuyahoga flowed from an act of journalistic malpractice.

That June 1969 "fire" was the thirteenth time the mightily-polluted Cuyahoga had ignited. The photos used by *Time* magazine that summer were from a 1952 conflagration that did serious damage to boats and bridges on the outskirts of Cleveland. The 1969 cover story caught the attention of voters, activists, and Washington insiders, but it was, to use a popular phrase from today, fake news.

All of this is ancient history to Mike, who is spending a few precious moments of his mother's final hours consulting with Nancy about how to deposit me at a good spot for hitching. We take a picture in the parking lot of a Bob Evans Restaurant and say our goodbyes.

I walk across the bridge over I-90, Cleveland's skyline off to the east, and set up my post just south of the Clinic on State Route 91. It does not look promising. Too many stop lights, which means that people exiting the interstate want to speed up to beat the light, not slow down to pick up a hitchhiker. It's uphill, without much shoulder for cars to easily pull over. Only the most dedicated rides will stop for me here.

It makes sense to move farther south. I walk three quarters of a mile up a steep grade, to an intersection at Chardon Road, a small commercial district. Most of the cars going by are folks heading home from work and starting their weekend.

My options here are several. I set down the pack and check my phone and learn that my friend Michelle has already alerted her considerable network of Buckeye State friends. One of them already purchased a pizza and some beer on my behalf and is ready to come get me once informed of my whereabouts. Simultaneously, I make a new Facebook friend, a marathoner named Shelby, who drove by, saw my hashtag and sent me a message promising to stop if I'm still stuck there when she came back around.

My friend Pat from Peninsula calls to check in on me. This is a huge change from the 1978 adventure, when the only way we could call someone would be to find a pay phone and call collect! Pat offers to come pick me up, but I am not ready to surrender. I tell him to give me another hour. He's a fisherman and has hitched many a mile, including long trips to Alaska. He understands how hitchhikers, like fishermen, always think that the next cast is going to net the big one.

Except, not tonight. An hour later, I purchase a six pack of New Belgium Fat Tire Amber Ale and a copy of the *Cleveland Plain Dealer* at the Shell station. My old friend Pat retrieves me and takes me to his home. It has been fifty-five hours since I walked out my door on Brown Gulf Road in Pompey, and I have traveled three hundred and fifty miles. Good thing this isn't a race.

"Hey, thanks, man," says the hitchhiker. "Thanks for stopping. Weren't you worried, that maybe I was a serial killer or something?"

"No," says the driver. "What are the chances of two serial killers being in the same car?"

# 7

## Red-headed Woodpeckers and Hitchhiking Serial Killers

You don't always know what brings a person into your path. Why did Morgan, the busy mother of a sick child, interrupt her drive, make two U-turns, and tack an extra hour of driving onto her day for the chance to help a stranger? Why did Mike and Nancy stop for me on a day that they knew might be Mike's ailing mother's last? How did Portia, with her pink shoelaces and heroin past, come to be leaving Denny's at the exact moment I was standing under that tree west of Buffalo?

Sometimes, though, you know exactly what it was. I crossed paths with ninety-nine-year-old Bill Toneff because of a bird.

The word went out from the cozy home of my friends Pat and Karin, tucked up against the Cuyahoga Valley National Forest, that a red-headed woodpecker had been sighted right off their porch. Bill, like my hosts, is a fanatical birder, and the red-headed woodpecker, chased by invasive starlings and shrinking habitat, is a rare sight. Bill hurried across the county to see for himself.

Bill had no idea that I was in the house. He has come with his field glasses to see the bird. Having spotted more than seven hundred distinct species of birds in his ten decades, he couldn't wait to see his first red-headed woodpecker. It is only the second time in twenty years that one has alighted outside Pat and Karin's house.

Bill and my hosts take turns gawking and commenting, analyzing the movements of the rare bird until he flies away, and Bill realizes there is a man in the room he doesn't know.

Pat introduces us, serves us both beers, and we sit in their dining room and talk hitchhiking. As a college student in the 1930s, Bill hitchhiked regularly from his family home in Lima, Ohio, to Columbus, where he attended Ohio State. He thought nothing of it. It was quicker than taking the bus.

I told him my own stories of hitching from Staten Island to Albany, where Joe and I went to college during the '70s.

Bill's father lost his butcher shop in the Great Depression, and his mother lost her job in a department store. There was no family car, no bus fare. Just his thumb. And it was never a problem finding someone to take him the ninety miles to school, and the ninety miles home.

Bill had almost finished college when he was drafted. It was during the Battle of Britain, before the US entered WWII. He started basic training one month before Pearl Harbor. On December 8, 1941, he was playing cards in the barracks at Fort Sill in Oklahoma, when President Roosevelt came on the radio and announced that the US was declaring war on Japan. A minute later, one of the soldiers reminded him that they only had twenty minutes left before they had to go back out to drill.

"Come on, deal the cards." They knew where they were headed.

As the war raged on, Bill was sent to Puerto Rico, to Fort Bragg,

Fort Mead, and eventually to Great Britain, always as a radio operator. He joined the Army's Third Armored Division, landing in Normandy three weeks after D-Day. Seventy-five years later, in a clear, calm voice, he tells me about what "magnificent soldiers" the Germans were, how hard his unit fought to push them across France and into Belgium and finally back into Germany.

"By the way," Bill says in that matter-of-fact manner common to men of his generation, "I was wounded twice." The Germans hunkered down, and when the time came for a big push to dislodge them, Bill was tapped as a forward observer for the assault. He would be the closest guy to the Germans' big guns.

"I was depressed," he tells me. "It was my lowest point ever." He was pretty sure his luck had run out, sitting in a foxhole waiting for dawn, when the field radio lit up with the voice of his battalion commander, a captain by the name of Snelling. (What a memory this man has!)

"You get the first furlough," the captain told him. "Thirty days at home."

"You're really serious?"

"I'll have a Jeep there before noon."

"It was the most euphoric moment of my life," Bill told me. "More than my wedding day." Bill had been married for sixty-eight years, until his wife died a year ago. "I thought I was the luckiest guy in the world. I'm gonna get out of this."

Shipped back to Paris, he waited with forty other soldiers for a transport plane headed home. "When the Battle of the Bulge broke out, they put furloughs on hold. We had to check a bulletin board in the hotel lobby every morning to see if we were going home, or staying put, or going back to the front. We went out every night. The French ladies were lovely. We drug ourselves back to the hotel, woke up in the morning to check the board."

On ten consecutive Parisian mornings, Bill and his hungover comrades staggered down to the hotel lobby to read a notice that their lives were still on hold, then went back to bed. After ten days of partying like there literally was no tomorrow, the morning blackboard message said they were shipping home. Bill and his comrades made their way to the airport and got that plane ride stateside.

And here's the thing. After surviving the Third Reich, getting shot twice along the way, and struggling through the years of the Great Depression, even Bill Toneff reacts with alarm when I tell him that I plan to hitch across the US. He's really worried for me.

"It's too dangerous," he says. He is more specific than most. He has a list of three reasons. "There's so much drugs, so much booze. And we don't institutionalize crazy people anymore."

No doubt about the drugs. Two days on the Heroin Highway made it obvious that opioids had moved in where factories moved out, creating a desperate subset of Americans compelled to do themselves and their loved ones great harm. But I don't think that junkies are picking up hitchhikers and doing us in.

What about the drinking? Bill is completely off the mark on that one. There is so much less drinking and driving than there was four decades ago. I can prove it both anecdotally and statistically. Checking my journal from the summer of '78, I find that on just one sunny July afternoon, Joe and I had hopped in the back of six different pickup trucks. Most of them were driven by men holding the wheel with one hand and a can of beer with the other.

That was the case more days than not. We carried with us the dominant, invincible young- male bravado of the era, assuming nothing bad would happen to us. Today I would be appalled, but then I remember feeling grateful whenever a driver reached into his cooler and handed us a cold bottle of Molson Brador or a can of Schlitz.

Yesterday, my last ride had come from Jim with the gun show bumper sticker, and in our half-mile ride he managed to tell me that he hadn't had a drink in thirty-three years. That would have been an embarrassing admission for a man to make back in the Jimmy Carter years.

Nothing has changed as dramatically in these past four decades as public attitudes toward drinking and driving. When we set out in the late '70s, it was legal to drive with a blood alcohol level of .15 percent. That dropped to .10 percent in the '80s, and by the turn of the century, all states had adopted .08 as the legal limit. The numbers tell the impact of this shift.

In 1982, alcohol-related automobile accidents killed 26,173 Americans. In 2009, only 12,744 of us were killed by drunk drivers. That's less than half the number killed in 1982, and in the same period, the population expanded from 231 million to 306 million.

Brief detour. I was nearly number 26,174. One February day that year, as I was pulling away from a red light on Grand Avenue in Phoenix, Arizona, a sixty-year-old man crossed a divider at sixty miles per hour and smashed his full-size Pontiac into my little blue Ford Pinto. He was drunk at eight o'clock in the morning.

His Grand Prix barreled through my Pinto, spinning it around three times, and then crashed into three parked cars in a used car lot. As I lay on the ground gasping for air, feeling blood run out of the side of my head and listening for the siren of an ambulance, I saw the driver emerge from his car, light a cigarette, lean back on the car and smoke, unharmed. I was lucky to survive with a bunch of broken ribs, some cuts and scrapes, and a collapsed lung. I spent three weeks in the hospital and two months out of work. Oh yeah— the guy didn't have insurance, either.

By 2017, in a nation of 325 million souls, the number of traffic fatalities had dropped further, to below eleven thousand. Between 1982 and 2017, the fatality rate per hundred-thousand people in the US declined by nearly two-thirds. Attitudes toward drinking and driving haven't just changed—it's a public health sea change, at least as big as the shift in how we view tobacco. Not surprisingly, I was holding a lit cigarette when the Grand Prix came down on me.

The notion of a designated driver was considered foolish and vaguely unmanly in the 1970s. Mothers Against Drunk Driving had not yet been formed, and many elders were still likely to wink and nod as they handed over the keys to their teenage miscreants. Uber was still beyond imagining.

I didn't have these statistics at hand as I sat with the genial Mr. Toneff, sipping a beer on a lovely Saturday afternoon in Ohio, talking about the dangers of hitchhiking. But I did have the word of Trooper RJ Smith of the New York State Police and two Onondaga County deputy sheriffs, each of whom had volunteered to me that drunk driving was much less common nowadays.

But what Bill said next got to the core of it. "The culture is so much more dangerous," he warned me.

The culture. The culture breeds fear and exaggerates the dangers we face. Yet fear is the dominant emotion in our personal and national lives. Where does all this fear come from?

From which crack in our national psyche does this misinformed fright ooze?

Fear of the unknown is innate. Born into each of us is a fear of the other—another species, another people. A startle reflex kicks in, puts us on alert, tells us to back away and survey our surroundings rather than to lean forward and embrace the new arrival. It's always a balancing act between that animal brain that wants to keep us alive to hunt one more day, to produce one more offspring, and the bigger part of us, our heart and soul, that wants to join in, to bond, to experience something even bigger than our tiny self.

On the road, when you see a hitchhiker, all these competing reflexes kick in at sixty or seventy miles an hour. What makes some of us stop and some of us keep moving down the road?

It is not about good and bad. I am certain that most of the people in the hundreds of cars that passed me on the roadside in Willoughby Heights were people who in their daily lives commit endless and sometimes heroic acts of kindness. I know this from the experience of my own town, where people volunteer countless hours to feed the homeless, run races and shave their heads for cancer research, shovel their neighbor's snow, and hold open the door for the next person in line. So why are we all so afraid of the stranger?

Outbreaks of goodness are a regular part of American life. When the author Philip Caputo towed his Airstream camper from Key West to the Arctic Ocean, he wrote with admiration about armies of nomadic volunteers he met in campgrounds and church parking lots all along the way. (See his 2013 book, *The Longest Road*.)

Yet, these acts often take place in structured settings. They are opportunities afforded to give connection, but within limits—toward ways of embracing the new and the frightening, minus the risk. These experiences are mediated, usually by organizations with liability insurance and multiple waivers to be signed before the dance or the cookie sale.

And frequently the participants return to their very different worlds, goods and services exchanged, prayers and hugs shared, while the calculus of vulnerability is unaltered, and the underlying social power dynamics remain in place. America has gotten "doing good" down to a science. What we've lost is the art of "taking a risk."

The hitchhiker/driver relationship employs no such intermediaries. It's you and me, me and you. Judgment, compassion, derision, hope, fear, wondering, recognition and the impossibility of recognition all tumble into view and out again at highway speed, landing splat on the pavement in a decision window that only opens for a few seconds. Luckily, I'm not asking the culture for a ride. I'm asking each individual who drives by.

And then there's fabled Billy Cook, the serial-killing hitchhiker, who spoiled the party for the rest of us. Billy himself seemed to think he was rotten. Surely the three adults, three children, and the dog he killed would be at a loss to find kind words for him. San Quentin's executioner who put an end to Billy in the gas chamber, in 1952, had no compunction about doing the deed, and the church in Missouri where his remains were sent, thought so little of miserable Mr. Cook that they buried him outside the cemetery fence and didn't even put up a stone to mark his grave.

Billy Cook might be the rarest of American outlaws, the hitchhiking serial killer, but he was the subject of a movie. The 1953 film noir classic, *The Hitch-Hiker*, directed by Ida Lupino, is faithful to the grim story of Billy's murdering spree, which started in Missouri and ended three weeks later when the *federales* slapped the cuffs on him in a Mexican fishing town. Billy's deformed face included an eyelid that never shut. His only real job was a brief stint dishwashing in California, and his few skills in life included dead-eye aim with a pistol and a keen sense of order when giving directions to the people he kidnapped, people he often drove around with for many sleepless days and nights before putting an end to them.

In the early 1950s, the radio was still the fastest means of news distribution, and Billy Cook's kidnapping and murdering spree gripped the country for weeks before he was taken down. The movie, to put it bluntly, scared the crap out of everybody. Lupino, who later went on to work for *The Twilight Zone*, knew how to make the heart skip a beat with every frame of *The Hitch-Hiker*. The shadows that follow Billy everywhere, the Hitchcock-like double bass rhythms, and the curt diction of the actors spitting out words like "grub" and "fella"— it's all grime and grit, and expertly ratchets up the fear quotient frame by frame.

The movie doesn't give you the backstory on Billy. He was born to a family of nine. His mother died when he was only five years old. His alcoholic father took the family off to live in an Oklahoma mineshaft. That went about as well as you would expect, and eventually Dad left them a bag of food and hit the road. The adoption agency managed to find a home for each of Billy's sisters and brothers, but there was no one to take in Billy, the ugly kid with the bad eye and the nasty disposition.

Billy found it easier to live in prison than foster care, so he spent his teen years breaking enough rules to get himself locked up. He had the words "Hard Luck" tattooed on his fingers. He beat up a guy in prison with a baseball bat, and still got out of jail. He hit the road and decided that robbing and killing worked better for him than cashing a paycheck.

If Billy were around today, the school counselors and the pastors would probably take notes to the effect that this child "has issues." Whatever his issues were, transportation wasn't central to the story of Billy Cook. Yet the salient detail to emerge from this movie, and others like it, is that hitchhikers kill.

The concluding episode of the first season of Rod Serling's *The Twilight Zone* is also about hitchhiking and is also titled *The Hitch-Hiker*. It features the charming ingenue, Inger Stevens, who plays a buyer for a New York clothing store. For some reason, she is driving her nice car across the country all by herself. She is startled to find a man standing roadside, wagging his thumb while she is having a flat tire fixed in Pennsylvania.

As she heads south and then westward, this strange man appears again and again on the side of the road, begging silently for a ride, and it starts to drive her mad. She is near the edge when she runs into and picks up a handsome sailor on leave, but by then she is behaving so erratically that even a presumably horny seaman bails on her.

Somewhere around Tucson, we learn that she has nothing to fear from the hitchhiker. She is already dead. Turns out, that flat tire in Pennsylvania caused a fatal rollover. The hitchhiker was a metaphor for death. But her cross-country trip was worse than death—it was fear.

The mid-seventies television series *The Hitcher*, with the famous tag line, "Don't Pick Him Up," was brought to you by the producers of *The Texas Chain Saw Massacre* and *The Amityville Horror*. So you can see how we hitchhikers got a bad rap.

We've yet to see the hitchhiker series about Gray, the dude on a motorcycle who drove young Joe and me, in separate trips, from the highway to his house, put us up and fed us for the night, then relayed us back to the highway the next morning. There is no TV series depicting the Frederick family of Lebanon, Ohio, who stopped, all three generations of them, near Oxford, Mississippi, in the summer of '78, and invited two bedraggled ruffians into their camper van, where we shared sandwiches and board games for seven hundred miles. The ones that don't kill anyone just don't make the news.

There's no podcast highlighting people like pink-clad Portia or Harmony's mother, Morgan, each who had the experience of sticking their thumb out into the wind because the alternative, the place and situation they were leaving behind, was far worse than what might lie ahead.

We've even forgotten that during WWII and Korea it was considered a patriotic duty to pick up hitchhiking soldiers and sailors.

From what crack in our psyche does this pervasive collective terror ooze? The capacity for fear is innate; the nurturing of it comes from the culture and the stories we share. Fearful people keep trying to tell me that my tribe has gone extinct. I hope to keep proving them wrong.

They've just seen the movies. I've been out on the road. Maybe tomorrow will be their day. I can be proven wrong by the driver of the very next vehicle that stops.

My birdwatching friends in Ohio decide it is best to drive Mr. Toneff home. He has partaken of a second beer, and we are no longer in 1978. I finish my own beer, an amber lager named for Elliot Ness, the Untouchable. It is time to pack and get ready to say goodbye to my old friends, Pat and Karin, and hopefully make some new ones.

# 8

## Jesus, Tuco, and Canned Fruit Cocktail

Who will pick you up? Everyone asks me that question.

Obviously, I didn't know the answer before I set out, but I got asked so many times that I decided to reply simply, "Ralph." Most people just stared at me quizzically, not sure how to respond. I get that a lot.

How could I possibly know how to answer when the answer was to be found in the future, out on the side of dozens of roadways? Who, indeed, will pick me up? The tease, the adventure, the allure of hitchhiking is that I wake up not knowing who will give me a lift today, and my ride wakes up not knowing who I am either.

Then we meet, and something new begins. It's like starting a new job or moving to a new town or kissing someone for the first time every single day.

You live the fears and the hopes that make up who you are, and somewhere inside, you choose to believe that the sunset will find you far from where you had breakfast. Or knowing that you might well be stuck in Omaha for the weekend. How you digest uncertainty, whether it scares you or excites you—that's part of what makes each of us tick.

I love the unknown. That's not to say that I don't fear it. I fear and love what is around the next bend, and I know that the only way to convert today's uncertainty into tomorrow's story is to get out there and live it. I set my feet in my boots, walk out the door, and stand by the roadside. It's not that difficult.

My own wife and another close friend assured me before I left Syracuse that under no circumstances would they ever pick up someone hitchhiking. That was not encouraging. I knew that the odds were against me. That's simple math. Hundreds and hundreds of vehicles will surely pass by on any given day before one of them stops. When that one car or truck slows down and pulls over to the shoulder, the feeling of triumph and elation that sweeps over me erases the hours of uncertainty and doubt that preceded it. It's a rush you can taste.

A hitchhiker cannot make the error of hoping with great specificity about how tomorrow, or even the next forty-five minutes, might evolve. To live on the road is to live in a stoic mode, stranded between glittering hopes and a disguise of chill apathy.

It's not the mileage or the timeline or the weather that make the whole thing such an enormous floating crap game. It's the characters.

Like Ricardo.

I had been dropped off at the TA Truckstop on Route 71, near Chippewa Lake, by John, a chubby forty-something bespectacled man in a Nissan Sentra. Like many of my rides, John had spent part of his youth hitchhiking.

Before his mid-life return to Catholicism, John had been a resident at a Zen monastery in Connecticut. These days, he is raising his ten children and conducting political research on statewide Supreme Court elections. From his comments on Pope Francis, I surmise that he is a very conservative Catholic and that his activism has mostly to do with outlawing abortion.

John offers me tea from his thermos. I decline this kind gesture. An offer of tea seems somehow more inviting, more intimate, than a cup of coffee. Many people I meet on the road reach out to offer me food and drink, fearful that I might go without. John and I would probably have plenty to disagree about if we were talking politics, but his genuine concern for me takes the conversation in a different direction.

John and his wife adopted two very sick babies. One was a four-month-old girl who died from a heart disorder. Boom. There we were. Me reeling still from the death of a granddaughter whose heartbeat I never felt, John still putting one foot in front of the other, though a child he loved had died so young.

Could you talk of politics with this man in this moment? I could not. We talk instead about hitchhiking. John has his own personal calculus, that it is possible to hitch anywhere in twice the amount of time it takes to drive there. I tell him I will keep that in mind. He drives past his home to take me to a truck stop he thinks has good possibilities for a long-haul ride.

People think that hitchhikers get picked up by truckers a lot, but this is rarely the case. John leaves me near a Country Pride Diner, where Samantha, on just her second day on the job, serves me oatmeal and coffee.

At the next table, a couple of truckers puzzle over the menu, discussing the calorie count of pancakes and omelets. Truckers discussing the nutritional content of truck stop food would have been a comedy skit forty years back, but today these burly guys are intently squinting at the menu, checking for trans fats. We've come a long way.

Samantha lets me take her picture but doesn't want it posted on social media. After charging my phone, washing up, and finishing my third cup of coffee, I make my way back to the roadside. I spend a quiet half hour near a red light just before the onramp to I-71, figuring this is a good place to catch a ride of a hundred miles or so to Columbus. I'm thinking I could get to St. Louis by tonight. Fool's plan.

The first man who stops is a sad character in a leather vest with a series of crosses dangling from his neck. He doesn't seem threatening, just needy. It's not violence that the hitchhiker fears. The real danger is this guy, the oddball or needy person you can't figure out. We really don't want to feel in the debt of someone, to be confined for a long time in a car with a person we just don't like. That's how I imagine a ride with this guy.

Why I judged him I can't say—just a Spidey sense. It's always a fine line between following your instincts and not letting your own biases take over. This was one call I didn't have to make. I was relieved to find out he was headed to Cleveland, the opposite way, giving me a graceful way to decline his too-friendly offer of a ride.

Then Ricardo stops.

At first, when his aged and creaky Freightliner pulls over I am slow to move toward the rig. I don't dare believe he is stopping for me. I have been fooled before by trucks easing onto the shoulder. On a ramp in Erie, I climbed the steps of the passenger side of a stopped semi, only to find a driver waving his finger, telling me to climb back down. He was busy filling out paperwork on his tablet.

The trucking business today, like any other business, is a corporate, data-driven  enterprise. Forty years back, more truckers owned their own rigs, and even fleet drivers looking for company would break the rules and give us a lift. Today their GPS tracks them to the tenth of a mile and cabin videos livestream their every move. For most fleet drivers, to pick up a hitchhiker is the same as asking to be fired.

But Ricardo is old school.

The side door flies open, crashing along its trajectory into the diesel muffler, a vertical cylinder with an exhaust pipe on top that swings back and forth as if on a hinge. I hear a voice that immediately sounds familiar, but I can't place it.

"I serve God!" booms the voice from the driver's seat. "Get in, man!

God told me to pick you up!" The man in the driver's seat roars in Tex-Mex-accented English. Ricardo reaches down, grabs my backpack, and lifts it high into the cab.

I scramble up the steps, my head just reaching the level of the seat. It is a long way up from the ground to the cab of a semi-tractor, and I make it up just in time to watch Ricardo flip my pack upside down and toss it into the compartment behind the passenger seat. He drops it on its head. My laptop, which sits on top of the pack, has just been crushed under the weight of all my stuff. I am tempted to pray that the God whose directions Ricardo follows with such specificity, would instruct him to be a little more careful with his passenger's electronics.

I get into the seat, thank the man at the wheel, and slam the creaky door shut. I turn around and maneuver my pack until it is on its side, figuring that there is no point in checking the integrity of the computer until the end of the ride. My attention turns to the non-stop flow of words coming from the man in the black sleeveless T-shirt.

His internal dialogue spills out and fills up the cab. Ricardo emits a torrent of words—a combination of religion, life story, and questions for me that do not wait for an answer.

My mind is overwhelmed, both by his effervescent embrace and the desire to figure out why his voice seems so definitively familiar. I have heard this man speak before—but where? Whose voice is this, who does it remind me of? It bugs me like a sliver of grapefruit stuck between my two front teeth.

And speaking of fruit . . .

"You want some grapes, bananas, bologna?"

I don't.

"Reach back and get me that can of fruit cocktail," Ricardo orders.

Unbuckling the seat belt, I fish around amidst the bags and boxes behind me until I feel something that seems about the size and shape of a can of fruit. I pull it out. Peaches.

"Good!" Ricardo is so loud, and the truck is loud, and everything about this moment is so loud, it made my head want to explode. I work every day in a gentle profession—massage therapy. For the past twenty-one years I have spent eight to ten hours a day in quiet rooms, where the only sounds are gentle moans of relief and the enchanting vocal solos of Enya. Ricardo is the soundtrack to somebody's life, but that somebody is not me.

"Open it!"

I do.

"You want some?"

I do not.

"Good! Then I can drink it from the can." And he does, upending the container and slurping it down. I am happy to be of service, mildly amused but also on edge, unsure what I've gotten myself into here.

This 1997 Freightliner cab is held together by zip ties and prayers, both of which Ricardo deploys liberally. To get in or out, you need to know what Ricardo calls "the combination." The door on my side only opens fully if you roll down the window, push the big cylindrical diesel muffler aside, and pull up on a zip tie threaded through the hole in the passenger side door, where the lock used to reside.

Ricardo's voice is jolting, but it isn't just the volume that is hurting me. Ricardo has a way of speaking that threatens to cause welts on my arm. Multiple times each mile he turns to me, taking his eyes off the road, and punctuates a new outburst with a backhand that smacks me on the arm. More than once he overshoots and whacks me square on the chest.

The truck bumps and bounces along, jostling its passengers and contents. Ricardo isn't quite sure what he is hauling—maybe some sort of fluid for automobiles? He doesn't seem to care.

He picked me up exactly one hundred and one miles east of Columbus. His destination is Florida, his home base nowadays, and the same place where he plans to: one, build a church; two, dig a lake; three, plant thousands of palm trees; and four, install a go-kart track for children, if I understand him correctly above the road noise, the engine growling, and the mezcla of Tejano pop and ranchera music, blaring at me from the satellite radio.

The windows are open. It is hot out and the truck has no air conditioning. Still the question— where have I heard this voice?

I send a text to my friend Michelle, a reporter, and ask if she can check prison records for the state of Wisconsin. Ricardo reports that he did hard time there and one night, in the depths of despair, the Lord had visited him and pardoned all his offenses.

His six kids and three wives—one Mexican, one black, the third a Puerto Rican woman, none ever mentioned by name—appear to be a bit more skeptical of Ricardo than the Lord. So far, they haven't rushed to join him at the altar of forgiveness. He tells me that he wants to give the rig to his son when he's old enough to drive, but the boy just won't return his calls. He can't communicate with his most recent wife because of a small matter of an order of protection.

That's okay with Ricardo because he understands that he did some things that will take some time to heal. "It's important for you to understand, Eddie, that I never killed anyone, and never used heroin."

There is some comfort in those words. I try to understand, but you must realize that this is a confusing way to offer comfort to someone you've just met. It's always good to hear that your driver has not committed murder, though it leaves you wondering why someone might choose to lead with that particular denial. Sounds like it was a combination of guns and weed and coke that got him seven and a half years in federal prison.

The music and the road noise and the sound of his coolers and packages rattle behind me. Ricardo tells me that he is one of fifteen kids in a migrant family that lived in twenty-four different places. "I've been driving and sexing since I was eleven," he tells me. "I was whooped as a kid. Imagine how I would have turned out if they hadn't whooped me!"

Imagine.

The springs under our seat creak like birds chirping in a jungle of roaring lions. Ricardo's voice growls through it all, filling the cabin and the moment with stories of an evil past, a dreamlike future, and the salvific moment in that federal detention facility, that instant that cleared all of history in one blinding flash of light. Jesus saved him.

Jesus and a Cuban guy in Florida who sold him this truck which, by his calculations, is earning him five thousand dollars on this one trip, which after expenses, including diesel and food and a ten percent tithe to the church, will net him twenty-seven hundred for three days' work.

Ricardo has the garbled diction and bump stock cadence of a rookie preacher. He and Jesus have gotten very tight in the crucible of deliverance and forgiveness that assures him of salvation and eternal life.

I've listened to evangelical preachers from Arkansas to Argentina, in both English and Spanish, and I know that there is always a climactic moment in their oration when their tale of a misspent youth turns to the glorious moment of redemption, and it's a process not very different from a sexual outing, at least from the male viewpoint, and following that somewhat icky metaphor, Ricardo is displaying an impressive amount of stamina.

Now, I have never done cocaine. Ricardo informs me that he has done plenty and sold plenty, along with tons of weed. But I have been told more than once that enough cocaine use can actually inhibit a man's ability to arrive at sexual fulfillment.

As Ricardo's ministerial fervor spirals upward and upward, building towards some unimaginable release, presumably in the form of an altar call featuring myself as the redeemed sinner, I begin to wonder if maybe he just isn't capable of getting there. His prayerful oratory goes round and round. As a potential convert, I both confuse and disappoint. By not surrendering, not turning my life over to the Lord of the universe, the one who has counted every hair on my head, a task which time is making easier with each passing day, I am keeping Ricardo stuck in this manic state. I am giving him the equivalent of evangelical blue balls.

Boom!

Suddenly I remember where I've heard the voice. It is not a comforting realization.

It's Tuco. Tuco Salamanca! Ricardo sounds exactly like Tuco, the craziest meth head among all the crazy meth heads that populate the cast of characters in *Breaking Bad*. Have you seen *Breaking Bad*? Tuco. Each insistent whack on my chest from the back of Ricardo's hand reminds me of the coiled violence inside Tuco, a streak of random that could go off like an amateur IED at any time. Ricardo is Tuco on Jesus.

I have known many a born-again Christian, and I count among them many dear friends. Ricardo sounds like he is in the "early Jesus" phase of his love affair with his savior, a phase in which he trusts that the voice in his head, which he equates with a man dying on a cross on a hillside long, long ago, will take care of every problem or situation he confronts. In this cosmology, I am part of God's plan, placed at precisely that spot on the roadside so that Ricardo can help guide me to salvation, and I can open his canned fruit cocktail.

In my limited experience, this honeymoon phase does not last forever, even among the neediest of the redeemed. Jesus, if we are to believe the scrolls that have been handed down, has limited patience with fools and is agnostic on the matter of consuming canned fruit. It has been eight and a half years since the Lord shed his light on Ricardo in a cell block in Wisconsin, eight and a half years since the old Ricardo died and the new one was born. But it's been just a few months since he's had a chance to practice his craft outside prison walls, which is what this truck cab is starting to feel like.

I have my map out, trying to figure where to get off to hitch to St. Louis. Then I start looking at Cincinnati, closer, and the Ohio River, and Kentucky, closer still. "Are you going through Lexington?"

Oh yeah, he'll take me there.

My friend Deb lives in Lexington. I send Deb in Lexington a text. "You free for dinner?" We are nearing Columbus, Ohio. Decision time.

The ramble continues. Ricardo had it good in prison. He knew how to handle gangsters. He grew up around them. He could have gone free after three and a half years, which suggests good behavior in the can. That behavior did not continue when he got out. He had spent too many hours obsessing about the pickup truck parked in his ex-wife's driveway. He went directly from prison to her house to claim his pickup, which violated the order of protection, and those pesky lawmen sent him back to finish his sentence.

I bump along in the truck just dying to hear this story from the mouth of his ex and his parole officer. And hoping to hear from Deb in Lexington or Michelle. Michelle later reports that she can find no record of Ricardo in the Wisconsin prison system.

Ricardo has gone quiet. He's turned off the satellite radio. "I'm sorry," he says.

I'm hoping the next sentence isn't about me and what he's planning to do with me.

"I know I hurt a lot of people. But that was the old Richard. He's dead. I've become a new creature in Christ." He's got his Bible along with him and he reads it every day. He says he is doing great as the new Richard.

I breathe a little easier.

"Except for one thing," he continues. "I haven't learned how to turn the other cheek."

I'm damned sure not turning mine.

Temporal matters matter little to Ricardo, who has a date with the Lord, a date set in a Biblical formula. He knows for a fact that Jesus is coming back within his lifetime, and that he will be raptured along with all the other saved souls. He is fully enamored of the Lord who has changed him and given him a new life. "I smoked weed from the time I was fifteen until I was fifty-three. Now I don't drink, I don't smoke, I don't womanize."

He just wants to get to Florida to plant vegetables and fruit trees before the rapture, so those who get left behind have something to eat. A noble thought.

His regular backhand whacks remind me that this is no street-corner lunatic preacher—it is a man whose hands are holding the wheel of the truck carrying me deeper and deeper into the South. His ultimate destination is my salvation. Ricardo is aching to claim me on behalf of the Lord.

A saving text from Deb, my friend in Lexington: "Sure. What time?"

We make the turn south on the arterial around Columbus, heading toward Cincinnati. An hour and a half later, we cross the Ohio River, and I'm chugging along the Robert E. Lee Dixie Highway in a Freightliner old enough to be Ricardo's grandbaby.

For today, for better or worse, this is the road.

And the "we"?

Today, it's me and Tuco, canned peaches and the Lord. You couldn't make this up with all the cocaine in all the prisons in all fifty states. Ricardo, man, today you are the answer to my unspoken prayer.

# 9

## Don't Be a Dick

Kentucky purrs.

The accent, the birds, the trucks humming by on the highway, the occasional prop plane flying over. It purrs slowly, like the voice of the ever-smiling cashier at the gas station near the strip mall where Ricardo left me off. Kentucky's greeting is just a tick slower than Ohio and issued far more frequently than back in New York. The hum is pleasant, like an afternoon buzz.

The contrast between the endless hyper spastic electric emissions coming from Ricardo's mouth for most of yesterday afternoon and this calm, sunny, warm spring morning—this purring eases my jangled nerves.

I walk the streets on the edge of Lexington with a sensation like that moment when your ear comes unplugged, hours after you've been swimming. The speed, the many noises of that truck, the height of the cab, and the bi-lingual Jesus patter mixed with jailhouse stories, all in a tight space and with no clear end in sight—I had started to get used to that, like you get used to feeling pressure on one side of your head and only hearing from the other side.

You can pour peroxide into your ear and hop up and down on one foot and bang your head with the palm of your hand, but after a while you give up and you almost forget it's clogged. Then the piddle comes loose with a trickle of warm water running down the side of your head, and life is good, and even if you're an atheist, you just spontaneously thank God that the dam has broken. Deliverance from Ricardo's fervor felt that good. It is a perfect morning for a walk in a town I have never seen.

My hostess in Lexington is the sheriff. It turns out that I was arriving just before primary elections were to be held. Deb has supervised or monitored voting all over the world, and she is the person in charge of keeping an eye on today's Democratic Party primaries in this county. Under Kentucky's electoral law, the person who holds that role is called the election sheriff.

This sheriff is a tiny five-foot-two redhead, but don't be fooled by her size. Deb Alexander, native of Kentucky, long time resident of Syracuse, citizen of the world, has been an election monitor in the Balkans, South Asia, Turkey, Kosovo, and now, of all places, Fayette County, Kentucky, where she was raised. A story I wrote about her a few years back, which is now framed and hanging on her townhouse wall, mentions that Deb Alexander spent more time in Afghanistan than any other civilian aid worker.

It would be hard to call what Deb does a career. She began traveling internationally as a Fulbright scholar, working in Calcutta with Mother Teresa. Then she got a couple of degrees from the Maxwell School of International Studies at Syracuse University. Sometimes, she gets a call from the Pentagon to fly off to conduct human rights training for Marines, and sometimes she volunteers with Habitat for Humanity, building houses for poor people in Kentucky. I'd call her a Renaissance woman, except that during the Renaissance, a woman of her intelligence and ability faced only two choices—either offer herself as property to a husband, or be charged with witchcraft and burned alive or drowned.

Since this is no longer the seventeenth century, and a single woman is currently allowed to own her own home, Deb invited me to spend the weekend. She lives in a townhouse with a spare bedroom. There is lipstick in the fridge, an Army helmet from Helmand Province perched on a cabinet and, hanging on the living room wall, a framed letter from Secretary of State John Kerry, thanking her for her work in Afghanistan as a civilian enlistee in the Global War on Terror.

On the night table next to my bed, there is a tea service. I don't drink tea in bed, but this genteel Southern touch tempts me to try.

During the day, while Deb monitors the election, I hang out with Mr. Mooch, a brown and white cat she smuggled home from Afghanistan after her last tour ended. Mooch knows how to turn on the water faucet to get a drink, a sign of high intelligence for an animal born in a place with no running water.

While the votes are being counted—the sheriff is only called when shenanigans are suspected—we seek dinner at an Irish pub called Ramsey's. A thick and sassy waitress named Cashie serves me a kick-ass Reuben and two pints of locally brewed Cougar Bait Blonde Ale.

Beer names, like the beverages themselves, have gotten so much more sophisticated since our 1978 pilgrimage. Joe and I were treated by my Uncle Bob to a tour of the Schlitz brewery in Milwaukee, an awe-inspiring site for two first-generation college boys. In Iowa, we discovered the aptly named Blatz, still the funniest name in hops, a light beer before the term was in circulation. Cougar Bait and its thousands of cousins across the land had yet to be conceived. Cougar Bait, I assure you, is worth the wait.

Joe and I touched down in thirty-nine states in the summer of

1978, but Kentucky wasn't one of them. I don't recall ever having visited the Bluegrass State. Kentucky being the Thoroughbred racing capital of the world, Deb took me on a tour of horse country.

She did part of her growing up on a horse farm. We lean on a fence and survey the house her family was permitted to occupy in exchange for caring for a pasture and the horses on the estate, which I guess made her a sharecropper's stepdaughter. We eat breakfast at the Keeneland stables and walk past the paddocks filled with the world's greatest Thoroughbreds being cleaned, groomed, and fed by ranch hands of every color, shape, and size.

If you follow national politics, you will note that Kentucky has been defined of late by two men—Mitch McConnell and the author, JD Vance. You probably know who Mitch is.

Deb, a lifelong Democrat, still refers to Mitch by his first name, and genuinely respects his understanding of his home state's history. She just can't figure out what in the Lord's name happened to him.

JD Vance is the author of *Hillbilly Elegy*, a 2016 memoir. Vance grew up in Kentucky and Ohio, and is now part of the Washington elite he enjoys mocking. He went to the right schools, got his ticket punched, and now works at a right-wing think tank. He's like the token white trash among conservative elitists.

His bootstrap story also helps Eastern white liberals think they understand those places they call the "flyover states." He helps people who subscribe to *The New Yorker* think they understand why Donald Trump got elected president, and for this they are grateful to him.

In Kentucky, reaction to him is a mixed bag. Vance gets a lot of grief for growing up in Ohio and writing about Kentucky. He gets even more grief for seeming to blame the dysfunctional aspects of hillbilly culture for the poverty of Appalachia.

In the Rust Belt, we are familiar with his kind—the guy who gets on the last lifeboat and then shakes his head and blames the rest of us for being too slow. In Upstate New York, we gin up a fair amount of resentment toward people on the coasts who don't get why we don't

seem to share their giddiness at the digital globalized world they
fly around.

You can call us slow if you like, but we're not dead. Last I heard,
elegies were for dead people.

My ride out of Lexington came from a real, live, proud hillbilly
tile mason named James. You're not supposed to have favorites, but
I have to say—I think James is my favorite ride out of a long line of
favorites. I mean, how can I not love Dave the surveyor for making
a U-turn to come back and get me on Route 20? Who wouldn't love
Morgan, the mom with a sick child, and badass Portia in pink for their
sheer daring and rip-roaring laugh-out-loud attitude toward their
far-from-easy lives?

But James. James! He just might save America.

Why do I say that?

James knows how to ask questions. He asks questions for the
simplest of reasons. He wants to know the answers. He talks like he
wants to learn something. He'd never make it on cable news.

James and his work partner, TJ, stop for me just a few minutes
after Deb drops me on the interstate, headed to Louisville. I am still
thinking St. Louis by nightfall. Turns out, James and TJ are headed to a
conference in Indianapolis, so my plans turn further north. One of the
first things James asks me is this: "What do people in New York think
about the guns?"

I give him my best answer. Something about him demands the
truth. I tell him it comes down to whether you live in a city or the
country. People in New York City and even smaller cities, like Syracuse,
don't want a lot of guns around because we see what guns do—they kill
people. People out in the countryside where I live want guns around
because they see what guns do— they kill animals. I'm the only guy on
my road who doesn't hunt. The only one who doesn't own a gun.

James listens.

Back home, my neighbor rounds up the hunting licenses of his
brothers and cousins on the morning that deer season starts in the fall,

and then heads up the hill across our road, in the dark. By the time I jog by his barn before breakfast, he usually has four deer carcasses hanging from the rafters.

I'm the son of a court officer and the grandson of a sergeant in the New York City Police Department. Both those men had badges and the right to carry a sidearm, and I never saw either of them packing. My father had no interest in guns. We were city people. You might call it a way of life.

This seems to satisfy James.

We spend a little bit of time talking about New York State, a place James and TJ have never visited, and don't know much about. They wanted to know about the attack on the World Trade Center. "Does everyone in New York hate Muslims?" James asks me, as we barrel along at eighty miles per hour on a section of interstate named the Pearl Harbor Memorial Highway.

No, I tell him. We don't hate Muslims. We do hate terrorists. I tell him about my cousin Lorraine, who died in the Twin Towers, and my brother-in-law, an Iranian-born Muslim. I tell him that a lot of families are like that.

James nods and keeps driving.

I ask about the ethnic background of most people in his small town and he answers in a way that made me wish this mason were a writer. There had only been one black guy in the county where he grew up, and as for the ethnicity of the whites, "People here been here so long they don't know what they are."

I love it. James still possesses a trait so many of us seem to have lost. He listens. He's not looking for categories, but for stories. It's real conversation, full of nuance and void of assumptions.

James quit school near the end of his senior year, to play baseball in Florida, and after he gave that a go, made his way back to Eastern Kentucky, the side he calls "the pretty part" of Kentucky, hillbilly country near the Red River Gorge. James and TJ lay tile for a company founded by Italian immigrant brothers who came over from the old country in 1927. He doesn't boast, but judging from the projects he's worked on, plus the fact that the company sent James to Italy to study for three weeks at the oldest stone masonry school in the world, I imagine he is pretty good at what he does.

TJ is on the quiet side. He smokes an occasional cigarette, while James, driving the Ford truck flawlessly, often removing both hands from the steering wheel to make a point, carries the conversation.

In between offering me bottles of water and telling me his moonshine recipe, James asks me his questions. He wants to know what the food is like in New York, what the staples are. He wants to know what my favorite food is in every place I'd ever been. He wants to hear about the pizza in New York. James and TJ are startled to hear that New York State has mountains and lakes, farms and small cities.

We are driving through horse country, leaving Lexington, and on to Louisville where they run the Derby and make the baseball bats. James assures me that the entire horse operation in Kentucky depends on Mexican workers. Thousands of them work on one ranch that's owned by an Arab sheik, who James thinks may be the richest man in the world.

He turns to me. I'm sitting on the passenger side of the backseat of the four-door pickup.

Hitchhikers the world over love the four-door pickup truck. It is one of the greatest innovations in automotive history. In 1978 it had yet to be invented, and consequently Joe and I rode in the beds of more than a dozen pickup trucks, which must be the most dangerous means of transportation this side of riding in the front seat with an actual serial killer.

Just a week earlier, on the side of the road west of Buffalo, I'd learned from Trooper RJ Smith of the New York State Police that, while it is illegal to hitchhike, it is still legal to carry passengers in the back of a pickup, as long as you are doing the speed limit and your destination is within five miles.

I liked James's truck a lot. He turns to me, his big hand over the back of TJ's seat, wrapped under the headrest, and asks a question. "Do you know how much courage it takes for these people to come here?" He is talking about the Mexican men, who work with him. I am all ears.

"How much courage would it take to walk four or five days across a desert? You get here, you don't speak the language. Our food is different. They're used to corn bread and pinto beans, and here we got fried taters. To come to a country where you don't know anyone, you don't speak the language, you don't know if you'll find a job. And you have to pay to get here! You could get sent right back. I'm not sure I have that kind of courage."

TJ concurs that their Mexican co-workers are a ballsy bunch. This conversation is causing me to toss out stereotypes as frequently as James spits chaw from his tobacco into the narrow neck of his empty plastic water bottle.

One friend of theirs, a co-worker who went by the nickname Chicken, has been with the company a long time. They know Chicken and his situation quite well. Chicken hired a guy to build a house for his family back in Mexico. Now the same guy is building another house for him, and one day at work, on his lunch break, Chicken was conducting business via cell phone with this compadre.

TJ and James were puzzled. "What is that language they're speaking?" TJ asked. "It's not Spanish," James concurred, but they couldn't agree on what to call this idiom, which even to their bluegrass ears did not sound like Spanish. They are very impressed with Chicken, both for his work ethic and the fact that he knew not one, but at least two foreign languages, and has learned enough English to cut and lay tile.

It might just be, if Chicken is from Central Mexico, that his family and friends speak Nahuatl, the Aztec language, or any one of the dozens of surviving indigenous tongues and their dialects.

"What would you call that?" asks James. "A language? A dialect?

Good question. Why were they asking me? I have spent a bit of time bumping around Central Mexico, but they don't know that. I'm just the hitchhiker, the guy from New York.

James makes up his mind. "It's like us and English," he says to TJ "They speak hillbilly Spanish."

TJ nods assent.

Hillbilly Spanish! That may be the most brilliant, beautiful descriptive phrase I have ever heard. Noam Chomsky, eat your heart out.

James may never have finished high school, but he learned a trade and he learned it well. Being a tile mason is not like being a coal miner. The miner lives with the fear that the value of what he knows can be taken from him when forces below the earth shift, or an economy he serves but does not control turns on him.

The mason carries his future in his own hands. James keeps up-to-date, and every day he practices a timeless art—like John, the guy who picked me up near Buffalo, who devoted himself to keeping blacksmithing alive, or Dave in the Finger Lakes, who loves his sailboat even in an age where there are so many faster ways to get across a body of water. The way I love spending weeks hitchhiking across a country, better than flying over it in four hours.

James is one of the smartest and most curious people I have ever met. The lilt of his voice is as lovely as some of the sentiments he utters. There is a sweetness you can taste in the way he speaks. His tone and cadence soothe as much as Ricardo's grates.

You can tell he's got a mischievous side. James told me that when he was in Rome, he snagged a piece of brick from the Coliseum and in northern Italy, drank grappa, which he described as Italian moonshine. On the return trip, he and his boss stopped in Paris to see the Louvre, only to find it closed. So, they went to Holland.

One night, in Amsterdam, he heard people speaking on a street corner in what he thought was Russian. He walked up to them and found out that they could speak English. To my knowledge, James speaks no Russian, but he did what he does.

He asked a question.

"Do you Russians hate Americans?"

"No, we love Americans," a man said in return.

"Coz in the US, they're always telling us that you all hate us."

James spent the rest of that night drinking with his new Russian friends. He's that kind of fearless. James has a way of viewing his own society and government with a critical eye, but he is no cynic. He takes responsibility for knowing and for deciding what this country he loves should be.

He tells me about his travels out west to Montana, which he considers the most beautiful place he's ever seen. The geysers, the mountains, the fishing, all left him breathless. Yet, even years later, he still feels a genuine sadness when he talks about Native Americans he met, people who looked lost, who were selling trinkets at their own gas stations, people he respected but who he felt had been robbed of their pride along with their land. James gets it.

A few years back, James ran for and won a seat on the local school board. Now if you are of a certain persuasion you might immediately be thinking creationism and tax-cutting. And you would be very wrong. James' big issue was funding for the arts. It ticks him off that every time the people want to save money, they come after the arts programs. What would a burly tile mason be without a good art teacher? Just a guy with a sack full of chisels.

Hillbilly stereotype? Knock yourself out. But those stereotypes wouldn't survive an hour in the backseat of the pickup that is taking me from Lexington to Lafayette. This is a guy who loves his place, and its customs and ideas, but he doesn't hate everyone else or, more importantly, feel threatened by ideas or customs that might differ.

He spits tobacco and explains to me the process by which one makes moonshine. He promises me a sample, which I am still waiting to enjoy.

Neither James nor TJ ever mentioned the name Trump. Nor did I. That truck ride reinforced my view that I should not let my bonds with my neighbors be contingent on my feelings and theirs toward any one individual, especially that one.

It is getting toward dinnertime as we drive through the heart of Indianapolis. Lucas Oil Stadium looms to the right. I text my friend Jennifer in Indianapolis, a food blogger and running friend and, last but not least, the Episcopal Bishop of Indiana. Jennifer is an African-American, born and raised on Staten Island. Female Episcopal bishops—that was definitely not a thing in 1978. I send her my regrets, and we motor on, bound north for another hour to the city of Lafayette.

The guys drop me at a Quality Inn. I get out of the truck and give them each a wristband. #NobodyHitchikesAnymore. I hand James a bumper sticker with the title of a song called, "Counting on Love." It's a love song the musician/songwriter Jess Novak wrote to her country just after the election results became known in November 2016.

Her lyrics talk about the division and fighting that preceded the election and continues non- stop right up until today. At the end of the song, she sings, voicing a sentiment that is equal parts hope and prayer: "People are better than we seem."

James likes that. He takes the sticker and gets all excited, starts fishing around in his truck, saying he had something he wanted to give me. He finds it. It is a small square sticker with a black background. Four words in white letters spell out his simple code.

"Don't Be A Dick."

"Kinda like the same thing," purrs James.

It kinda is. Don't be a dick. Be like James. Counting on Love.

# 10

## Tilting at Windmills

I had an easy time getting out of Lafayette, Indiana, in a pickup driven by Steve. Steve is doing roofing these days, but he takes what he can get. "Anything you can do to a house, I can do," he boasts.

Lafayette is a town on Interstate 65, halfway between Indianapolis and Chicago. In Steve's telling, Lafayette was a sleepy town that began to wake up twenty years ago when it removed the railroad line that divided downtown in half. This interests me, because Syracuse is facing a decision this year about what to do with the Interstate Highway that cuts our town in half.

Steve says his biggest problem is finding workers for all the roofing jobs he has. When he stops to pick me up, he is on the way to work on the multi-million-dollar home of a car dealer who, according to Steve, puts twenty thousand dollars a week into an account for each of his grandchildren. I'm not sure how many grandchildren he has, but it sounds like each of them starts each new year with another million in the trust fund.

Steve has no trust fund. He works through pain every day. Yesterday, he had a cortisone shot for a trick knee. His doctor offered him opioid painkillers, but he declined. He's a small businessman in a prosperous economy in Mike Pence's state, and yet he volunteers, in a whisper, that he is not a fan of Donald Trump.

He has his own take on things. "I'm a Democrat, but not a liberal Democrat. I don't like all these handouts; everyone should get out and work." Mostly, he wishes he could find more workers to help handle his roofing business. He likes hearing talk of infrastructure improvement, but he is embarrassed by the president's behavior and "the way the government is being run lately—taking from the little guy and giving to the big guy."

We are driving through Trump country, a state the Republican ticket won by a nearly twenty percent margin over Hillary Clinton. Clinton got beat twice in Indiana in 2016. She also lost the Democratic primary to Bernie Sanders.

I exit Steve's truck on an off-ramp, just ten miles from where he picked me up. He offers me water and reminds me: "Be safe out there."

When I give Steve a wristband and the sticker that says "Counting on Love," he looks around, casting his eyes side-to-side before he replies.

"I'm counting on Mueller. Good luck to you."

Back in 1978, a handsome twenty-two-year-old named Chuck, who was cruising through Michigan with dark hair and sunglasses, driving a brand-new white Volkswagen Rabbit, stopped to pick me and Joe up in Lansing. He took us west to Ludington, where we hopped an overnight ferry across Lake Michigan to Wisconsin.

Chuck told us that his father was an airline president. We had no reason not to believe him.

We spent a delightful couple of hours with him and he drove us right to the dock—a nice guy. I only mention him because he came to mind, following the class-conscious Steve's discussion of his roofing client's socking away money in his grandkids' trust fund. Chuck may well have been a trust fund baby, the only person I recall of his social class, who gave us a ride in that summer of '78.

Chuck was about my age, and I hope that today he is happy and doing well. What neither of us could have imagined back then is how increasingly rare it would be, forty years later, for ordinary working people to mingle on an equal footing with people of his class. The industrial heartland, where air conditioners and washing machines, automobiles and refrigerators were built, has since collapsed in on itself. Union jobs with good salaries and reliable benefits had become the exception to the rule.

Back in 1978, we drove past factories that we assumed were like the mountains and canyons of the West—immutable features of the landscape. Newspapers, mainstream churches, and teeming factories have all been washed away, their bones like fossils with no one to study them. Indiana still hangs onto a share of industrial production, but many of the good-paying jobs that built the middle class have moved to Mexico, or are performed by robots.

In 1978, a CEO made, on average, thirty times what a line worker could earn. Today the ratio hovers closer to three hundred to one. Today, kids like Chuck, the children of CEOs, may not even know that hitchhikers exist, or that we ever did.

Speaking of jobs replaced by robots, I had generally assumed that the occupation of hitchhiking is safe from automation. In other words, I did not think I could be replaced by a machine. Then I heard the story of HitchBot, a robot dressed up to look like a cross between the cowboy in Toy Story and R2D2 from Star Wars. This little guy, invented by a group of Canadians, hitched across Germany, the Netherlands, and Canada before coming to the US, making it as far as Philadelphia before getting mugged.

Someone in the City of Brotherly Love beheaded the HitchBot, ending the Canadians' little experiment. I am sure nothing like this will happen to me, as I am planning to avoid Philadelphia.

I liked listening to Steve the roofer, but now I'm stuck on a ramp with a bad lie in West Lafayette. There are a lot of trucks, and it's an uphill grade leading to a long bend before the highway. Any eighteen-wheeler pulling onto the ramp here is thinking of acceleration, not about stopping for me. The driver probably wouldn't even see me.

Everything in hitching is about the spot, and this is a lousy one. A lot of families come by, probably picking up university students at nearby Purdue and, while they are friendly and many wave to me, they keep going.

I have sort of a routine when I get to a new spot. I spend the first ten to fifteen minutes with the pack on my back, doing mini dips to strengthen my legs. Then I walk up and down with the pack on, facing traffic and holding my sign out.

When my shoulders start hurting, I find a signpost to help me set the pack down. I lean into the signpost backwards, unbuckle my chest and hip straps, slip my arms from inside the straps, and slowly slide down with the pack gliding along the signpost. I grab the top of the frame to break the pull of gravity as it lowers the pack to the ground.

Early on, I just let my arms out of the straps, but I found that the pack pitched right backward and landed on its head, where my laptop resides. I don't want to risk breaking another computer.

I forgot to tell you. The moment when Ricardo tossed my pack into his truck was the end of the line for my little Dell notebook. Neither thoughts and prayers, nor the helpful technician at a Best Buy in Lexington could revive that computer. Fortunately, the young man directed me to a cheap one on sale for two hundred dollars, and Deb the sheriff was kind enough to wait around. With the help of my Visa card, I was back on the road and on the internet.

A Google Maps car drives by with that strange rotating camera tower on the roof. Somehow it worries me. Thousands of vinyl-wrapped

Hyundais are now roaming the globe shooting images with seven or more cameras, creating those street-level images you can find when you go to Google Maps. If I'm stuck on a ramp long enough to be uploaded to Google, that can't be good. (They didn't update that spot until July, and I wasn't in the picture—good thing.)

It is getting hot. The geography is not favorable. The ramp to I-65 North curves around to the right, so sharply that even if a car wants to stop, a driver could reasonably fear being rear-ended by the next vehicle coming around the bend.

Two sweltering hours later, Chip comes along. Chip is a thirty-six-year-old nurse. He doesn't usually take this route, but today he is bringing work supplies to his father. Dad has a business that treats industrial wastewater, but Chip does not see himself as mechanically inclined, so he went into the medical field and works with heart patients at a local hospital.

He asks permission to smoke, and then lights up a Pall Mall. In 1978, nobody asked if it was okay to smoke. They just offered you one of their cigarettes.

Five minutes into the ride, we are engulfed by giants. Giant windmills. Thousands of them, from east to west, and as far north as I could see. Chip says they've been here for ten years and now he barely notices them.

I sure do. Last time around, crossing the Midwest was a profound monotony on a par with trekking across an Iraqi desert. The Midwest was acres and acres and miles and miles of unending agricultural tracts. Now it is miles and miles and acres and acres of unending agricultural tracts peppered with enormous wind turbines—white, three bladed, whirling generators, which you either love or hate or, as in the case of Chip, barely notice anymore. He lets me off in Remington, where US Route 24 heads west.

Trent is the kid cleaning tables at McDonald's. A blond boy in his late teens or early twenties, he is thorough and pleasant and eager to please. We get talking about life in Remington, Indiana. Trent lives with his parents and probably always will. They drive him the two miles to work and back.

Trent tells me that I'm the first hitchhiker he's seen this year. Last year, he saw a few. I'm not sure what Trent's issues are—he's got a limitation, but it's not Down Syndrome. He doesn't have the single crease in the palms of his hands that all those special ones carry. I'm thinking that forty years ago, we would not have made room for a kid like Trent to work at McDonald's. Kindness moves forward, even in cruel times.

McDonald's has been a haven for hitchhikers for as long as I've been thumbing rides. Bathrooms, free water, shade, air conditioning, electricity to charge a phone, wi-fi to check on the world back home—what's not to like? Plus, they now serve the Egg McMuffin all day long.

McDonald's is, for better or worse, a melting pot of cultures. People come to America now already knowing our brands, with Coca Cola and McDonald's running through their veins. In the McDonald's on Route 24 near Remington, I overhear conversations in Russian, Chinese, and Spanish Indiana. In yuppie coffee shops, sometimes the only international flavor is the macchiato.

Ten minutes after I say goodbye to Trent, a sturdy man with dark hair and a beard picks me up in a Subaru. Gary works at the Subaru plant in Lafayette and is proud of it. Before that, he worked erecting pole barns and was proud of that. His forearms and wrists are thick. He just finished his shift, smoked a joint (the scent of the dube still lingers in the car), and is heading home to clean house and make dinner for his girlfriend and kids. He loves cleaning his house and making dinner for his girlfriend and kids. Gary is just a happy guy.

Indiana's economy has always been more diversified than some of its neighboring states. The collapse of manufacturing doesn't sting here in quite the same way it does in Michigan or Wisconsin. Guys I meet here, like Gary and Steve the roofer and Chip the nurse, and even Trent the busboy, can always find work.

The turbines are good for the economy, but Gary thinks they're wasteful. Their electricity is being shipped to New York, he says, a great inefficiency. Not exactly. This forest of turbines we are driving through is part of the Amazon Wind Farm Fowler Ridge.

You wouldn't know that from any signage, but this stretch of northern Indiana is home to one of the largest wind farms in the nation, and it powers the internet. Amazon is not only in charge of delivering those little boxes with the strangely comic-erotic logo to your door, and publishing *The Washington Post*, they also control a huge portion of "the cloud" through their subsidiary, Amazon Web Services.

The cloud needs a lot of juice, and a chunk of that juice comes from Indiana wind turbines. When someone mentioned the cloud back in 1978, they meant it was going to rain. Now it means that some farmers in Indiana get to lease acreage to Amazon to make energy from wind. That may sound cool to you and me, but to Gary, those big white giants are just an eyesore.

He misses seeing the sunset. Gary can't look west from his house and see the setting sun without being distracted by all the blinking lights on the turbines, which are required to make the turbines visible to airplanes.

My next driver scoffs at Gary's sensibilities. "When I get home from work," says Adam, who stopped for me on Route 24 at the edge of Kentland, "I'm too tired to look at the sunset."

I had walked the length of the quiet town of Kentland, past a barber shop, the jail, and the Newton County Historical Society, which was closed. Nobody seemed bothered by me, but no one stopped for me either, for an hour or more, until Adam pulled over.

It is hot. Inside his Ford Escape it seems even hotter. Adam is a burly, black-bearded guy with a story as twisted as this rural two-lane highway is straight. Today is his first day on a new job and he's gotten a nasty sunburn. He is working with a crew, building a grain elevator. It's a temp job, paying fourteen dollars an hour. Before that, he was working indoors at a pallet factory. And before that, he worked for a month in Biloxi, Mississippi, replacing insulation in a casino, until Hurricane Nate came along with 125-mile-an-hour winds.

"I've had a lot of good jobs," says Adam. "I've lost a lot of good jobs."

His love life sounds like a bit of a hurricane. Adam tells me he's just been dumped by his girlfriend, but that the love of his life is a woman in Peoria with whom he shares a platonic relationship. His most recent ex just had surgery for liver cancer, or so she says. She has a small child she recently produced with another man, lives with her parents and her new boyfriend, and so, understandably, there are some trust issues.

The liver-cancer-ex calls Adam while we're driving. It isn't on speaker phone, but I can hear crying. She is begging him to bring her cigarettes. He listens, then argues, admonishing her, finally relenting. The scent of co-dependency fills the Midwestern air.

The phone call ends. Adam narrates his life story. He was born in California. His father was from Bangladesh, but he's never met him. Adam came to Indiana as a nine-month-old baby, he's been told, on the only airplane flight of his life. People love to pick up hitchhikers and tell their life story. I have the greatest job in the world, I think to myself. Listening to strangers.

I should say that, for the most part, I am relating their stories as told to me. I'm the  hitchhiker, no longer a reporter. But sometimes the stories beg verification. Such was the case in Colorado a few months back when, on a short hitching expedition with my son Rob, a man named Dale gave us a twenty-minute ride in a decrepit minivan and told us that he had once been a botanist working for NASA, developing plants that could be grown on the moon. When funding for the space program shriveled, Dale switched gears and started teaching hydroponic marijuana cultivation to Rocky Mountain cannabis entrepreneurs.

Rob and I got out of the van convinced that Dale was as creative with the truth as he was generous with his vehicle. Until I googled his name. Sure enough, he had been featured in *The Atlantic*, profiled as the scientist behind High Altitude School of Hydroponics (HASH), a pioneer in Colorado's premier lifestyle industry.

But back to Adam. He once spent a month homeless, living in his car. That seems to be the wellspring of his empathy. "People who stop for hitchhikers are people who know what it's like," he states with assurance. The closest thing he has to a parent these days is the mother of one of his ex-girlfriends.

I try to keep up with the timeline of his chaotic life, picking out every other word over the blaring satellite radio in his ancient Ford Escape. The soundtrack shuttles between country music and rap. I will forever remember Adam as the man who introduced me to the genre of country rap, a.k.a. Hick Hop, the only place on YouTube where you will see a Confederate flag in a rap video. At least I hope so.

We pull off Route 24 and wind through the gray streets of the tiny town of Watseka, just over the Indiana-Illinois border. Adam describes the place he now lives as a town with lots of drama and lots of gangbangers. It looks run down, but I don't see any gang graffiti on the walls of the abandoned houses, for what that's worth.

He pulls into a driveway. A heavyset woman in a loose-fitting, sleeveless white T-shirt emerges from a beat-up house, an implanted IV port visible below her clavicle, the port's catheter dangling. I presume she is Adam's ex. She apparently isn't kidding about cancer.

He waits in the driver's seat for her to make the walk up the driveway. She cries and apologizes and cries some more, clutching his forearm through the window.

He lights into her. "You know your family is the worst people I ever met, don't you?"

She nods.

"Straight-up trash."

She continues to sob, looking at the pack of smokes in the breast pocket of his T-shirt. Adam tells her she had better stay away from the drugs, whatever that means. He gives her two cigarettes, puts the car in reverse, and backs out.

As we drive away and get back on the road, Adam's mood improves considerably. Out of the blue, he offers to drive me to Peoria, the city where his soulmate resides. I'm bewildered and not sure how much of this is true, but if my next best option is to get out and take my chances in Watseka, I'm all ears.

Adam tells me that only recently has he learned how to start taking care of himself. He's practicing his new skill set. He will take me to Peoria if I can buy him some aloe vera lotion for his sunburn and chip in some money for gas.

That sounds like strange currency, but it is late afternoon and this hot, flat land isn't showing me any better offer, so I say, sure, why not, Adam? And it's off to Peoria, two hours away through flat lands planted with soy and punctuated by cool little towns with names like Gilman and Crescent City, towns that surprise me by how much they look like they could be in the Adirondacks.

As we make our way along old Illinois Route One, cutting corners I never saw on the map, Adam endeavors to explain life to me. A hitchhiker is many things, but we are always a captive audience. "Our society," he drones, "is way worse than it used to be. We don't care about each other. People say they feel bad, but they don't help you. They expect the government to give you money."

There's a blues song on the radio now: "Tennessee Whiskey." Part of the chorus goes, "You're as smooth as Tennessee whiskey/You're as sweet as strawberry wine."

Adam has a warm spot for the working poor. "I know people who work and don't make enough to take care of their kids. People who work in group homes for sixty hours a week and it isn't enough." Group homes and social services seem to be a big part of the economy of Watseka.

Adam is very upset that the government keeps wanting to cut public-school funding. "That's a big mistake—that's the future of our country."

"Pass Me a Cold One" blares from the dashboard speakers. So, I ask him, what does he want to do about it?

Anything but vote. As eloquent as he is about our social ills, Adam never votes. He's not a fan of Donald Trump, but can't be bothered voting since, in his view, it's only the Electoral College that matters.

We skirt the edge of Bloomington, Illinois, past the beautifully landscaped corporate headquarters of State Farm Insurance. Adam has switched from cigarettes to a vaping device and I can't tell what's in it.

We pass a garage sale sign. "Classy Crap for Sale." We don't stop. Just outside Peoria, traffic is held up by a police drug checkpoint. There's a K-9 deputy and a sign that says, "All vehicles are subject to search." They just wave us on.

We arrive in Peoria as the sun sets. I feel bad for Gary back in Kentland, because the sunset here is indeed picturesque. I buy Adam some gas, get him some lotion at the drugstore, take his picture, and we say our goodbyes outside the Quality Inn. He's happy. Happy like it's payday, he rides off to meet his soulmate.

Peoria had a reputation as Anytown, USA, a test market for products and performances. It dated back to vaudeville days, when theater companies, musicians, even comedians, Groucho Marx among them, liked to try out their work in Peoria to see if it caught fire.

Richard Nixon's advisor, John Ehrlichman, would later say, "It will play in Peoria," to indicate that a policy would be popular nationwide if it were popular here at the edge of the Midwest. For a time, Peoria matched the nation's demographics and politics closely. The same could once be said of Syracuse.

Politicians could and did use Peoria as a proxy for how they were doing. Those days are gone. Adam packs a ton of hurt and a bundle of challenges, but don't count on him to vote, in Peoria, or anywhere else. He's got his sunburn and his soulmate to take care of, and a full tank of gas to get him to work tomorrow.

I covered nearly two hundred Midwestern miles today, mostly on secondary roads that gave me a closeup look at a lot of small towns. We talked about energy and health care and education and got a close-up look at disability, addiction, health care, obesity, and infidelity. Did I leave anything out?

I check in at the Quality Inn, to be honest, feeling less than eager to see what Peoria in daylight has to offer. Hopefully a nice, long ride.

# 11

## Lightning and Snakes

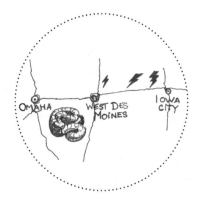

Sprawl. Goddam sprawl. Ramps, ramps, ramps.

When you know someone in a town, they set you up with a
good spot. Sean, my friend the writer back in Buffalo, had driven me
fifteen minutes out of town to find just the right place on Route 20,
in Hamburg. Without him, I might still be thumbing my way through
downtown Buffalo. Pat and Karin, my bird-watching Ohio friends, had
picked a spot on I-271, headed toward Columbus, that had a great flow
of traffic. In Lexington, Sheriff Deb deposited me in a prime location
and along came TJ and James within minutes.

I have no friends here. The closest I have to a friend is Adam,
who in his eagerness to bond with his soulmate offered no useful
information about Peoria whatsoever.

All I can see out the motel window is a tangled knot of interstate ramps.

On top of that, it is raining.

Cities used to have a beginning, a middle, and an end. Now they stretch on forever. Even a smaller city like Peoria ambles on endlessly, exit after exit, making it hard to distinguish urban from suburban from the middle of nowhere. Cities are thinning out and getting poorer, while suburbs stretch on and get richer. There are more poor people, and fewer people overall, in our cities. And for the hitchhiking clan, there's a bewildering choice of ramps.

I take a chance and set up on a ramp for 74 West, headed toward Galesburg. Never heard of Galesburg before.

Cars fly by, accelerating up the ramp. This is just the morning rush hour crowd, I reason. An hour goes by and a breeze kicks up, chilling me in my wet, short-sleeved shirt. Peoria people can't be all that different from Syracuse people. I'll get a ride.

What could possibly go wrong?

Then the lightning starts. The clouds open up, and it starts thundering.

I run as fast as I can with that pack on my back. I will later learn that the word peoria comes from the original inhabitants of the area, the Illinois, and in their language, it literally means "he who comes with a pack on his back." By the time this wet peoria gets to the parking lot of the Northwoods Mall, there is an inch of water covering the parking lot and it is running like a river.

I dash inside the mall and catch my breath. This is no passing shower. In the center court, a furniture store has set out a nice living room display. I take advantage of the couch, spreading out my belongings to dry.

Before anyone can object to my presence, I walk over to Auntie Anne's Pretzels and order three pretzels and a Coke. I sit myself down on that couch to indulge in a sodium and sugar orgy. There is a skylight above, which will let me know, with greater accuracy than my phone's weather app, just when the sun comes back out.

I read my book. I check email and Facebook on my phone. I pull out my laptop and write for a while. I find a newspaper and read that. Two hours pass and I am almost dried out. The rain has ceased and, while it isn't sunny, the clouds are starting to thin.

The rain delay has given me time to learn a little bit about Peoria. Like Syracuse, Peoria is a city built on a lake. Both Onondaga Lake back home and Lake Peoria right here were nearly killed off by industrial pollution. Only in recent years are they starting to come back to life.

Syracuse suffered the loss of our biggest industrial employer, Carrier Corporation, a decade ago. Peoria is now watching Caterpillar crawl away, taking with it as many as fifteen thousand jobs.

Peoria is the fastest shrinking city in a shrinking state. Its urban core is poor and diverse, the suburbs whiter and intent on staying that way. Feels like home.

It's two in the afternoon when I get back out to the road. I try a different ramp, one coming in from a feeder road, just to the north. I left my hotel six hours ago, hitched for four of them, and I can still see the place where I woke up. Peoria and I are not getting along.

Cars keep coming up the ramp, dozens every minute, but no one is in a mood to stop. I can't really blame them. There isn't any great place to pull over. I feel more raindrops. Then a big flash of lightning strikes, followed by another, and then another deluge comes on so quickly that I can't outrun the river pouring along the curb of the onramp.

I climb over a guardrail and sprint across a patch of grass back in the direction of the hotel. There is only one break in the fence, about two hundred feet ahead of me. I keep going, squeeze through with my backpack, and find refuge under an awning outside a different hotel lobby.

One of the nice things about being a white guy is that you can pretty much wander into private property without being noticed or impeded. I have this routine that I've used so many times as a journalist that I have a name for it. I call it my White Guy Thing. If you are of the belief that racial equality has somehow blossomed in our land, I invite you to watch me do this thing sometime.

The White Guy Thing has helped me get backstage with rock stars, into summits of presidents, even once into an art auction in New York where tickets sold for three hundred dollars, without paying. It's a manner of moving forward, nodding to the security guys like I'm giving them permission to be here.

I can teach it to you. First you have to be white.

Even soaked like a rat, wearing an ancient backpack, my smile and complexion charm a nice lady exiting The Residence Inn. She kindly holds the door open for me. I had absolutely no business being there, and the staff had every right to boot me out.

I walk up to the desk and ask for the Wi-Fi code, take a couple of mints from the candy dish, and saunter off in search of a restroom. Dylan's words filled my head. Come in, she said, I'll give you shelter from the storm.

In the men's room I pull my shirt over my head and spend the next half hour shaking it under the blow dryer and sticking my head into the warm airflow to chase the chill and dry my hair and clothes. I emerge borderline presentable, though a tad musty. The weather is still miserable.

Outside it's hot, humid, and rainy. Inside it's dry, but chilly from air conditioning. I'm not sure how long I can hang out in this lobby pretending to be waiting for someone.

This is when I start to hear the voices of all those people who have been telling me for the better part of a year to "Stay safe out there." Mostly, they were warning me about dangerous unnamed humans. I worry more about lightning.

The storm shows no signs of letting up. I decide to follow their cautious advice. I summon Melvin.

Melvin is a retired electrician. He's also an Uber driver. I had only used Uber twice before this trip, but I have the app loaded on my phone for just for such an occasion. Melvin, I ask the app, please take me to the bus station.

Melvin is opinionated. Melvin is unpleasant. Melvin is a great argument for self-driving cars. I tell him what I'm doing, and he responds that he would never ever pick up a hitchhiker. He goes the extra mile, letting me know that he would never stop even to help someone with a flat tire. If they don't have a friend to call, they just aren't the kind of person he wants to be around.

Then he veers into the bizarre. "I think these people are making me sort of racist lately," says Melvin. This totally unsolicited comment came out of left field, prefaced by the obligatory exculpatory observation that almost half of his passengers are black.

"These people" are making Melvin racist. Just giving him no choice in the matter, as if racism were a respiratory infection that you can pick up just by breathing.

Melvin is getting himself worked up as he drives. I'm in the front seat next to him. He's big, and bald, and loud. He drives with one hand on the wheel and both gums flapping.

"It's all this stuff they're asking for—reparations and everything! And that Starbucks thing— they knew before they went in there, before they did that."

I think he is talking about an incident in a Starbucks, where a manager had two black patrons arrested. My understanding is that the Starbucks customers went in to meet for coffee.

There is no stopping the Melvin train. "And now that we have Trump in there, they've gotta let him do what he said he was gonna do!"

Okay. As a guest in someone's car I am obliged to be a polite audience. In this case, I am the paying customer, and Melvin is putting his politics on full display. I've worked on twenty thousand people in my career as a massage therapist, and not one of them has gotten a political speech from me while paying for their service. I can't figure out how to de-escalate his diatribe.

"You like Trump?" I ask, and immediately feel silly.

Melvin does something I will never forget.

He takes his right hand off the wheel.

He thumps his chest.

"Trump! I AM Trump! Trump IS ME!"

He thumps his chest again. This is leaving the realm of politics and entering the world of the DSM-5 Manual for mental disorders. Melvin's rant continues with his highlight reel of the offenses committed in the Obama/Clinton era.

"Get rid of the nine-and-a-half-billion-dollar deficits Obama ran up!"

"Put all these people in jail!"

"That Hillary has blood on her hands. She took all those security guards out of Benghazi."

My head is hurting. But I'm taking notes.

Before getting out of that cab, I ask him one question. It is hard to pick through the maze of misinformation, but since he brought up Benghazi, I ask why he thought she would do that.

He looks puzzled. "Who?"

"Why do you think Hillary Clinton, as Secretary of State, would take security guards away from a consular office?" (She didn't.)

"I have no idea," says Melvin, as if he'd never thought about it. And he seems to slow down for a second. He pulls off the highway and starts to navigate city streets.

As we pull up to the bus station, Melvin regains his footing and leaves me with one parting thought. Melvin tells me what he plans to do when it is his time to die. "I'm going to get a bottle of whiskey, crawl out of the house on a winter day, lean up against a tree, guzzle the booze, and freeze to death." He has arranged to donate his body to science, because, he informs me, "It is the only way you can die without paying for it. They cut you up for three months, then cremate you and send your ashes to anyone who gives a shit."

Well, that's one less funeral I have to attend.

Some have suggested to me that hitchhiking is something like

Uber. They miss the point. For one thing, you pay for Uber or Lyft. Hitchhikers get free rides. Kindness requited, and on rare occasion, aloe vera lotion and a tank of gas is the only reward. And when you get out of the Uber, they ask you to rate the driver.

I rated Melvin "terrible." I love hearing people's opinions, even ones I disagree with, but I am a paying customer, Melvin, so keep all that vile noise to yourself.

Melvin is the nightmare scenario for those of us out on the road. There are very few serial killers out there, but a good number of assholes. The only good thing about the ride with Melvin was its brevity. But, like Gollum in The Lord of the Rings, even Melvin had his part to play in my journey. He took me to downtown Peoria, where I saw things I would never have seen from the interstate.

One final thought before I go into the bus station.

In 1978, with the exception of one old Mississippi farmer in a pickup dropping the N word, we did not hear this kind of blatant racist talk. In 1978, there was plenty of racism to go around, and the north was no better than the south. But it was a moment when you at least had to act, outside your own tight little circle, like you were trying. Now it's more like open season. Angry white men feel free to let it all out.

Remember the Klan talk in the bar back in Erie, Pennsylvania? I didn't go there looking for racism. I was looking for a pizza. The racism found me. In Peoria, I wasn't seeking out a bigot— I was looking for a ride, and Melvin's hatred found me.

The moment in 1978 we hitchhiked through, was a nation rehearsing new lines, reading a different, unfamiliar script. Practicing not talking and acting like racists—that counts for something in a country with a history of legally sanctioned discrimination, segregation, and worse. That is the genius of some great religions, including the Catholic one I grew up in, or grew out of, as I sometimes say. Every Sunday you say the same things and everyone around you says the same thing, and if you are saying good things, the right things, maybe when church is over you will have learned to say and do the right thing by your neighbor, because you just heard them pledge to do the same. Maybe.

Blocking the narrow entrance door to the City Link bus terminal, three addicts, hands in pockets, lean over, clothes and hair all a wreck, not barricading the door, just weaving around in space so =there is no easy way to get by them. Then one of them opens the door for me. I thank him.

The inside of City Link buzzes like a hive. A moving clot of humanity covers all the seats and most of the floor. There are sounds coming from under blankets and inside jackets, but I can't say that the noise rises to the level of language. It is more like a hum. It doesn't take long for me to realize that this is not just the Greyhound station, but also the city bus depot and the gathering place for homeless and mentally ill people.

It is a scene from hell, but in truth, it is a scene that makes me far more comfortable than the prison nightmare of riding in Melvin's Uber.

At least a dozen meth heads are sitting and standing, mostly standing, arguing in terms that make no sense, at least to me. In this way, Peoria is backward compared to Syracuse. Meth is so "2015" in our town. Our current epidemic favors heroin, oxycodone, and fentanyl. Peoria's addicts seem hopelessly behind the times.

They sit on piles of clothing and blankets. They point, but not at anything I can see.

A middle-aged woman with strong arms and enormous, deep, beautiful, steel-grey eyes has a hand on the right side of the belly of another, noticeably pregnant woman. Into an audio landscape layered with rumbling moans of withdrawal and a chain of psychotic call-and-response dialogues, this serene lady whispers enchantments.

She cups the baby bump of one very troubled mother-to-be and rolls her eyes as if in a trance, calling on her version of the divine to bring this child out of this hell and into a better world. I can't take my eyes off the pair. In this community of desperate souls, this woman appears to have a vision for herself. She has found her role.

On this day, she is the depot's reiki master. Tomorrow, she might be the midwife.

I sit in a plastic seat not ten feet from her, taking notes and keeping my pack close by, strapped to my leg, and I think of my granddaughter Caroline and wonder about the life that awaits this child of the depot.

The reiki treatment ends abruptly as a police van pulls up. Two officers, one male and one female, emerge. They come inside and grab a middle-aged woman by the arm. They search her pockets and her bag, then escort her toward the van. She moves slowly, her head bobbing up and down.

After a decent interval inside the van, both cops re-emerge and come back in to arrest a man. He does not go easily. They take him to the ground amidst a commotion, and what pops out of his pockets gets the attention of the men and women around me. Crystal. The man being apprehended, a chubby white guy, cannot make words come out of his mouth. He doesn't have much fight in him, but he is trying his best to get free of their grasp.

A third officer, a very large man, enters, and soon they have the guy cuffed and in the van. For the rest of the hour or so I spend there, the female officer, who seems to be in charge, interviews the other occupants of the bus station, asking for their testimony on the arrest. To most of the homeless it seems like just another normal day. This is their daily reminder to stay in their lane.

Outside, city transit buses come and go. Two kinds of people descend the stairs. Those with purpose in their step, people headed home from work, and others who amble or mope across the lobby, with no urgency or apparent direction. Fair to say that the city of Peoria has decided that the bus depot is where they will concentrate their poor and homeless during the day, keeping them out of sight of hard-working taxpayers.

What struck me most about Peoria's bus station was how carefully it was set up for me not to see it. Like most of our society's setup, organized around automobiles, choices, and mobility, we can avoid all the unpleasantness that we can afford to avoid. Urban design in America has always had a genius for segregation.

The section of town where I had been hitching unsuccessfully all day resembled the northern suburbs of Syracuse, and probably most towns in between. Highway ramps, big box retail stores, few pedestrians. The houses were large and new and, by somebody's lights, pretty. The cars had air conditioning and tinted windows. The drivers were busy people with much to do.

I'm not sure I ever would have gotten a ride out of there unless I had paid Melvin.

These folks downtown at City Link had little to do, no urgent need to get anywhere, and all the time in the world to wait. The young man behind me in line for the bus was on a work release program and was headed back to spend the night in a state prison. I was going to spend the night on the Greyhound bound for Omaha.

I felt defeated as I boarded the bus. No ride, no prospect of a ride.

But the Greyhound offered a place to sleep cheaper than a motel. And I wouldn't have to wake up tomorrow in Peoria. My day there taught me this—that if I ever have to choose between Uber Melvin's chest-thumping tribe and the lost souls lining the walls and floors of the bus station, I know where I hope to stand every time.

My only regret—and you may never hear another New Yorker say this—is that I won't get to hitch through Iowa, a state that holds a special place in my heart. In the summer of 1978, Joe and I had hitched into the city of Ames, Iowa, to call on a former girlfriend of his. I use the term "girlfriend" here generously. Joe had met Hope Ann on a high school Easter break in France and fallen madly in love with her.

Their romance consisted of torrid letters he composed to her from Staten Island and a brief visit we made to her daddy's farm after graduating high school. During that visit, Joe came within inches of proposing marriage to Hope Ann and sending me home on a Greyhound to break the news to his family. Joe was an impulsive youth.

I never got Hope Ann's version of their Parisian amour, or the time they spent together in Ames, but I did spend many nights on long distance phone calls later that year, talking Joe off the ledge after Hope broke his heart. Viewed from the perspective of forty years later, three marriages and five kids between us, it seems silly that Joe would have given that farm girl a second thought. But sure enough, when we planned our post-college hitchhike through America, Joe wanted us to be sure to make a stop in Ames.

So it was that, in August 1978, a lovely Iowa family picked Joe and I up in Madison, Wisconsin, and took us all the way to Iowa City in a Chevy sedan. A short hop later, we were close enough to Ames to call Hope from a public pay phone.

To my surprise but not Joe's, she was happy to hear from us. Hope Ann sent her husband to fetch us from the highway. I can't remember the guy's name now, but I do remember passing a VW Bug in a ditch and him telling us that Hope Ann had just totaled the vehicle the week before in a collision with a sow that had crossed her path after dark. It was a double loss—they had equity interests in both the sow and the Beetle.

Hope Ann was sitting on the porch when we pulled up. She did her best to greet us without rising. Both her arms were occupied, bottle-feeding a pair of piglets, the now-orphaned offspring of the sow that had gotten the better of Hope Ann's Beetle. Times were tough for the small-scale hog farmers of Iowa, and the man Hope had married in the intervening years couldn't afford to lose a litter and a productive sow in the same season. Hope Ann, noticeably more ample than during her Paris days, held these little piggies as they suckled for dear life.

Hope and her husband were gracious and hospitable hosts, and they put us up for the night. As they showed us to our room upstairs, all I could think was, "Joseph, all this could have been yours."

Still in Peoria, I crawl into the Greyhound, shaking the scent of defeat and embracing the relief of a pair of seats, side by side, all to myself. I am beat. I can't remember how many times this day I have been wet and dry and wet again, but I am pretty sure that if you lined up every car that had passed me by on the Peoria roadside today, they would stretch to Chicago.

The Greyhound smells terrible, like someone removed the air fresheners and replaced them with used disposable diapers.

I fall asleep and don't wake up until the bus pulls into Iowa City, waking with Uber Melvin still in my head. Something he blurted out suddenly comes back to me.

It was just as he rejected my offer of a wristband, the only person on my trip to do so. In a burst of delusional optimism, I showed him the website written on the wristband and told him he could follow my trip online. He shook his head. "I've never touched a computer."

And in the darkness of the bus heading west through the Iowa night, with nothing else to think about, I wonder—how did this guy manage to sign up to drive for Uber?

# 12

## Nebraska Was Always Tough

"I Go By Johnny" did eight years in the Army. He's fifty years old now and lives, for the moment, on a slab of cardboard behind a utility substation, a short walk from a busy McDonald's that is the last stop before getting on the ramp leaving Omaha. Johnny is working the off-ramp from I-80, and I'm hitching the on-ramp, looking for a ride west. I cross six lanes of traffic to see what I can learn from him, to get the lay of the land.

It's been hours standing here and the sun is high in the sky. The thermometer on my phone says it's already 92 degrees. On the asphalt ramp, it must be closer to a hundred degrees. Johnny tells me that my chances for a ride here are not good. "This is a rich neighborhood," he says, and we both know what that means. "Nobody stops here."

Johnny says he will take a ride anywhere, but what he's really seeking are donations.

We have all seen Johnny. Back home I pass a dozen Johnnies every day. We don't want to give him money because we know he'll spend it on drink. This Johnny says he needs something to drink and fifty bucks for a room. He hasn't slept indoors for days and is in serious need of a shower.

Johnny confides something to me, about the giant Catch 22 in the life of every guy holding a cardboard sign at every urban intersection across America. "I have to drink to do this," he says.

It is hard to beg. It is humiliating. To take the shame of begging for beer money away, he must get drunk. And when he gets some coin, of course, he drinks it up, sleeps it off on his cardboard bed, then finds his way back to the ramp, which is where we are talking now.

His story meanders. Eight years in the Army. Fort Smith, Arkansas. Riverside, California. Three kids. His only family is his mother, who lives Lincoln, Nebraska. Three months ago, Johnny got hit by a car. To get his broken wrist fixed, he had to hitch to California to retrieve his birth certificate. "HUD and food stamps require it," he tells me.

Johnny says that he drinks but doesn't smoke weed. Then a guy with his windows rolled down pulls up to the stop sign at the end of the offramp. His girlfriend waves and gives Johnny an enthusiastic hello. The driver hands him a joint and asks him how California was. So, Johnny's a regular here.

A black guy, who doesn't want to give me his name, comes down the hill, leaning on crutches. His right leg below the knee has been amputated. Johnny starts packing it up. He's giving the man, a fellow veteran, his spot. It's automatic. Respect. Man's gotta have a code.

I'm ready for a break from the heat. Johnny follows me into McDonald's. I buy him a breakfast sandwich. The friendly lady at the counter looks at me, then looks at Johnny, then back at me with a subtle shake of the head that says, "I hope you know what you're getting into." McDonald's cashiers are the bartenders and paramedics of urban

America. They've seen it all, they don't get rattled, and they move on to the next customer.

In my pack I carry raisins, a chunk of summer sausage, and dozens of Wild Cherry Life Savers. In a side pouch I have a bottle of water. There have been a few times when nibbling on the sausage has kept hunger at bay. For everything else, there's McDonald's.

I know that I can find healthier food, and I should support local restaurants, but thus far, none of those healthy locavore establishments have set up anywhere near the ramps and roadways that I've been living on the past two weeks.

I've eaten more Big Macs and Egg McMuffins since leaving home than I will ever confess to my doctor. I have swallowed at least a gallon of McDonald's coffee, which the people at the counter will happily refill for you without charge. I go to McDonald's, not the local church, when I need to fill up my water bottle with clean, cold water. I brush my teeth in the men's room, splash cold water on my face, charge my phone in the outlet near the booth, and use Ronald McDonald's Wi-Fi whenever the signal is strong enough. It usually is.

McDonald's is my oasis. And this one is packed.

If you use the drive-thru, another great American invention that keeps the haves and the have-nots from rubbing elbows, you get quicker service. But when you sit in the two-tone plastic seats, America just comes to your table.

I see a team of high school volleyball players lining up with their coaches for a celebratory meal before heading home. I see migrant workers climb out from the backs of trucks and form lines out the door. I watch families parceling out french fries to the kids to make their funds last for the ride. I hear a dozen or more languages.

In McDonald's, truckers and bikers and grandmas have watched out for my belongings while I used the rest room, and I've returned the favor more than once. On this busy roadside, which might seem like the most transient of places, McDonald's is a pop-up community center.

It's a place for Glenn to rest and wait out the heat. Glenn's a bearded wisp of a man who has been riding the rails and cycling the country almost non-stop since retiring from the Navy in 1993. He's got a bike locked outside and he's waiting for the day to cool, trying to decide between riding east, or spending fifty dollars on the Econo Lodge across the street.

It's a place where practical considerations force multicultural cooperation, where over the din you hear an Anglo manager call out to a new hire, "Yo necesito french fries!"

It's the place where Jimmy and his new titanium hip re-entered the work force after four years on disability. He and his wife still sell their blood plasma twice a week to cover the bills. Two times a week is the maximum that even vampiric private donation centers will stick a needle in your arm. The Red Cross only lets you come once a month, but Jimmy likes being back at work. He wipes my table and offers me a ride ten miles down the road, if I'm still here when his shift ends.

McDonald's is a day-care center and a drop-in center for the mentally ill. One little girl, maybe ten years old, is at a different booth each time I come back in, sometimes sitting, sometimes sleeping. Her mother, who can't possibly afford childcare on McDonald's wages, works behind the counter.

I see a middle-aged woman, her red hair perfectly pulled into a bun at the top of her head, come in and out ten times in the space of a few hours, picking a different seat each time, pretending to talk on the phone, acting like she is waiting for someone. She goes out to her car for a little while, waits for the crowd inside to turn over, then makes a new entrance to the same place she spends all day, maybe every day. The staff know her deal, and still she gets treated just like anyone else.

These are the snatches of McDonald's life that I glimpse in between my shifts, standing on the roadside at the edge of Omaha. Every two hours, I have to get out of the heat. My water bottle nears empty, mostly from pouring it over my head, and my sunscreen starts to lose the battle with the insistent, scorching sun rays.

Toward the end of each shift, I tell myself that I'll wait another hundred cars. After counting to a hundred, I strap up and walk back to the Golden Arches to be greeted by my new friends. By now, I have told most of the counter people my story, and they are wearing wristbands saying, Nobody Hitchhikes Anymore.

I buy something each time I stop in, and I try to be polite. I'm heaving my pack into a booth when a tall, sandy-haired man asks me about my sign and where I am going. He and his daughter are on their way to church and then to a basketball tournament. "Her game is at two. If you're still out there, I can take you about two hours west of here."

And that is how, finally, after a very long, hot day, I get out of Omaha. Thanks to Scott, a Mennonite basketball coach from Henderson, Nebraska. And thanks to the Golden Arches. In the late afternoon, a good five hours after Scott and I spoke in McDonald's, I was feeling desperate. I walked far down the ramp, edging close to the roadway, increasing my chances of getting busted. At this point, I'm thinking that if I have to spend another night in Omaha, I don't care if it is jail. Nebraska has always been a tough place to get a ride.

In 1978, a state trooper kicked Joe and me off the road in western Nebraska, near North Platte. His name was RJ Thompson. He gave us warning tickets and threatened to haul us in if we left the ramp again. We didn't know much about Nebraska. This was four years before Springsteen made Nebraska a household name with an album that included two cop stories.

I imagine that if Officer Thompson is still alive, he is long retired by now. I start to wonder what he's doing, maybe fishing in Florida. Just then, an old brown Buick pulls over. It's Scott! A man of his word. Scott opens the trunk of the car and invites me to put my pack in.

Mesa, his daughter, is sitting in the front.

"So, did you win?" I ask.

The team lost by three points. Mesa did not play. She turned her ankle in volleyball practice. Scott and his wife have five kids and each one of them, like Mesa, is a three-sport athlete. Scott has been a coach his whole adult life, ever since he finished his own college basketball career. He's been a farmer and now he sells insurance, but the family is devoted to two things—their God and their games.

Scott is fifty-two and comes from a small Mennonite community in central Nebraska. He lives twenty miles from where he grew up, near the farm his father and grandfather worked. Though he will routinely drive four hours to Sioux Falls or Wichita or Kansas City to take one of the children to a game, he has never been on a train, nor been east of Richmond, Indiana. He met his wife at Hastings College in Hastings, Nebraska, where they both played basketball.

I ask Scott why he picked me up. Having a teenage daughter in the car is enough to make any man decide that picking up a roadside vagrant is somebody else's job. Many a mother would hit the roof, if she heard from their daughter that Daddy had picked up a hitchhiker while she was in the car.

Scott's calculus is just the opposite. "People need help," he said. "If my daughter were on the side of the road with a flat tire, I hope someone would help. It's just the right thing to do."

People need help. People are more vulnerable than dangerous. For Scott, it is as simple as that. He tells me about the sermon preached at church today. The pastor encouraged his flock to be "doers, not just hearers" of the Gospel. That type of Gospel seemed deeply engrained in Scott, who had made his offer of a ride hours before he heard the preacher. He is coaching Mesa.

Just like "I Go By Johnny," this man, too, has a code. Scott drives his daughter two hours to a tournament she can't play in and makes sure she goes to church before the games begin.

Scott and Mesa take me past their exit and leave me at the entrance ramp near Aurora. My new friends think this is a better place for me to catch a ride west. Miraculously, a little white Toyota slows down just after the Mennonites drive away.

I hope that this is my ticket to Denver, but as I run to the car, the young driver holds a dollar bill through a narrow opening in the passenger door window. It is a strange dance. As I approach, he wiggles the dollar and inches forward. He looks at me as if he wants me to take the money. The window is barely cracked. He has no intention of stopping.

"I don't need money," I cry, trying not to shout. "I just need a ride to Denver." He pushes his offering one last time, shakes his head, then pulls away. I'm not a bum. I don't need money. I'm not a hobo, either.

There is a distinction, by the way. Bums beg. They don't work. Hobos work to travel. A tramp can be either a bum or a hobo. But I'm not a bum. I worked hard to get here. That sounds strange, I know. I can still see that young man's face. I don't want his dollar. Even more than a ride to Denver, I want to know what is behind that fear I saw in his eyes.

I am not quite sure where I am, but I know that I've been out in the sun for a long time today. I need a pair of trees close enough to one another to string my hammock, but there isn't a tree in sight. It's western prairie grasses, nearly knee-high, going on for miles and miles. I walk up and down the ramp, trucks and cars going by, sun dropping toward the horizon.

I call Ellen back in Syracuse. My phone screen is so scratched, and the sun is glinting off it. Hard to see. She checks Google Maps for me. No good news. Even a satellite can't find me a place to lay my head.

I spend another hour on the roadside, hoping some kind prairie person comes along to cleanse my soul from that weird interaction with Toyota dollar-boy. It isn't working. Nebraska has confounded me again. I don't want to give up. The memory of what happened next in North Platte, all those years ago, makes me smile and want to keep on hitching.

Not long after officer RJ Thompson had read Joe and me the riot act, a recreational vehicle had stopped. The door opened, a shaggy, young dark-haired man called out, telling us to climb in. That ride took us almost a thousand miles, all the way to Idaho Falls.

That won't happen this time. As much as I don't want to give up on Nebraska, she is giving up on me. I do not find a ride that night, but

I find a stationary kindness in the person of Brodie, the manager of the Arby's at the Love's Truckstop on the eastbound side of I-70.

Walking the mile to that Arby's, I scope out a spot on the prairie about fifty yards from the road. The grass slopes down enough to provide a modicum of privacy, and I pat down enough of it so that I can settle my hammock and sleeping bag on the ground and fashion a comfortable enough place to rest till dawn. Then I check into the Arby's to wash up and eat.

Before I order my sandwich, Brodie announces that he is giving me a ten percent discount for smiling.

I am not aware that I am smiling. In fact, I am surprised. Then I catch on—he is giving me a senior discount and dressing it up by calling it a break for smilers.

Brodie, as pleasant as all the Great Plains, insists that no, he is the manager and has the discretion to offer anyone a discount for any reason, and that mine is solely for smiling.

I like Brodie. I offer him a wristband. He is happy as anyone I've ever met. Brodie worked in restaurants in Montana until his wife missed her family in Nebraska so much that he moved here and found work, just to keep her happy. He promises to come to my table for a picture. A few minutes later, he hops out from behind the counter, and we conduct a full-blown photo op.

He asks me what I would like to watch on the TV, and he tries his best to find the NBA championship game, but the truck stop's cable subscription does not include ABC.

I pull out my computer and start to read up about the prairie that I was about to spend the night on. Brodie appears once again at my table, announcing that it is "turnover time." Setting down a pair of warm apple pastries, he pulls up a chair and sits down to join me. A church-going man with evident joy in his heart, he pauses for a prayer before we consume the pastries.

I mention my intention to camp out under the stars across the road. He does not see wisdom in my plan. He sees snakes. In late spring, warm dry prairie days lead to chilly dry prairie nights, and creatures lying on the ground can feel pretty cold. I wave him off, noting that my sleeping bag can keep me warm down to fifteen degrees.

I'm missing his point. Brodie gets up to go back to work, and he mentions the prairie rattlesnake. The venomous viper would be seeking out a warm spot to pass the cold night, and my warm-blooded body in a mummy bag will be very inviting. And so, I leave Aurora, Nebraska, on the midnight Greyhound, with a warm pastry in my belly, and a memory and photo of a new friend.

Lightning and rattlesnakes. Melvin back in Peoria. There are still a few things out there that can scare me.

*"For all those shut down strangers, and hot rod angels*
*Rumbling through this promised land*
*Tonight, my baby and me, we're gonna ride to the sea*
*And wash these sins off our hands."*

—Bruce Springsteen, "Racing in the Street,"
*Darkness on the Edge of Town, 1978*

# 13

## Bacon Broccoli Slaw

The first time I ever saw the Rockies was from the front seat of a Holiday Rambler. It was July 28, 1978, the morning after Officer RJ Thompson of the Nebraska State Police had invited Joe and me to get off the interstate.

That day, hands down, was the most annoying wait for a ride we had endured all summer. The temperature rose to a hundred degrees. Twenty-mile-an-hour winds blew dust at us, burrowing into our pores, our noses, and our cracked lips. Forty years later, I can still close my eyes and taste the dirt on the roof of my mouth.

The sun burned so hot, I didn't want to keep my eyes open. The sounds were even worse. One thing you learn if you stand exposed on a prairie long enough, is that the chirp rate among crickets rises along with temperature. That escalating racket is a sure-fire recipe for driving a pair of Eastern city boys insane. We could sleep through sirens wailing and TVs blaring, but the two movements that make up the chirp of a cricket, multiplied a million times? That just didn't happen in the boroughs.

The only break from the North Platte cycle of cricket chirping was the distant and hopeful hum of a car approaching us, lifting our spirits briefly before whooshing by in a great dust devil of disappointment, then tailing off into a cruel silence, occasionally punctuated by the prayers and curses Joe and I launched into the prairie. Then the cricket chorus took back the stage.

We took breaks and lay down next to our packs, seeking illusory shade where there was none. We took futile turns waving at the travelers ignoring us. We got mean. We gave up, but there was no one to accept our surrender. And then the Holiday Rambler pulled over.

The Holiday Rambler was a mid-sized motor home, a class of vehicles we cursed and ridiculed, both for their extreme gas-guzzling nature and the fact that no one driving a motor home ever stopped to help a hitchhiker. Until July 28, 1978. Until Terry.

When the massive rolling home pulled to the side of the road, we didn't believe he was stopping for us. Until the back door opened, and another guy named Brian waved us in.

"Quick!" he admonished us. "Got any weed?"

We did not, but they let us onboard anyway.

Terry was driving the RV from the Rambler factory in Elkhart, Indiana, to a dealer in Idaho Falls, Idaho. As day turned into night, and the camper rolled on, Terry picked up and dropped off a small brigade of hippies and vagabonds, most of whom brought weed to the mobile jam fest in exchange for the ride.

Joe and I had only our company to contribute to the party, that and my passable versions of the few obligatory Fogelberg, Steven Stills, and Carole King songs that shy boys at state schools learned to strum on guitars back in the seventies. I was no lead guitarist, but I could pluck well enough to make stoners smile and help some of my friends find romance.

The RV stopped only for gas and hitchhikers. It came equipped with a toilet and drinking water, everything we might need. Terry the driver pushed on through the darkness, displaying a practiced stamina that outlasted all the partakers, including Joe, who found a few square feet of floor space and crashed somewhere passing east of Pine Bluffs, just before we crossed into Wyoming. I rode shotgun.

We traveled through Rock Springs, a crazy mining town bursting at the seams, still looking like the days of the wild, wild West. By the time we got to Idaho Falls, where Terry splashed water on his face in a gas station and put on a tie to deliver the Holiday Rambler to the unsuspecting dealer, it was eight in the morning. He had driven all night and was about to catch a plane east, to go fetch another RV. For Joe and me, it was time to figure out a way to cross the Tetons.

All that to say that we never made it to Colorado in 1978. We skirted just to the north. This time, I will make up for that. My younger son Robert is finishing up his last year of a Ph.D. program in Ecology and I am taking the opportunity to visit with him in Fort Collins. He knows more about weather and plant species in the prairies out this way than you can fit in a doctoral dissertation, which is what he's working on. He also knows how to find the fun and the beauty in wherever he lives.

Robert had been a somewhat unenthusiastic participant in a dry run for this cross-country trip of mine, a few months earlier. I visited him in April and asked him to spend a day on the road with me, hitching, when he would have rather been rock climbing. Four rides in three hours, and we made our way to Boulder, getting our final lift from an adventurous bartender named Melissa, who took us to a sports bar where we watched a bit of the college basketball tournament called March Madness.

Dale, the guy who told us he was running the school for hydroponic weed production that prompted a fact-check, was another one of our rides that day. That afternoon spent on the road was a small sample of twenty-first century hitching, but enough to give me and my son some encouragement that somebody would get me across the country.

Rob has a lot of interesting friends in Fort Collins. On this second visit, I stay in the house he shares with two other men, a dog that looks like Spuds Mackenzie, and a Marmoset monkey by the name of Bubba. One afternoon, we go down to visit Bubba in the basement. Bubba is the Melvin of monkeys. He has a very violent reaction to meeting men. He throws fruit at me. I withdraw.

The rest of Fort Collins is much more welcoming, and Robert and I spend a good bit of the next few days visiting brew pubs and coffee shops. On my last morning, we eat an enormous breakfast at a Cajun place called Lucille's, which is famous for its beignets. I'm not a big beignet fan, but the coffee is excellent.

After breakfast, Robert drops me at a spot outside Fort Collins, where the road north to Laramie intersects Highway 14, a two-lane state route that leads west into the Rockies across the Poudre River Canyon. I can tell that Rob is a little worried about leaving his old man alone at the edge of a mountain range, but he's even more worried that I'll stick around—he's got research to catch up on. It's been a great visit but it's time to move on.

Highway 14 is a steady climb through mostly national forest lands, with a few little outposts sprinkled here and there. My first lift out of that little spot is from a plumber named Rick, who moved here from southern California with his third wife, to afford grazing land for his horses. There's plenty of work for a plumber but not enough help, he offered, repeating a familiar refrain. We climb a hundred feet or so in elevation over twelve miles of the Poudre Canyon Highway.

Rick lets me out at Mishawaka, a restaurant, tavern, and riverside music amphitheater. Rob has told me that this is a great place to enjoy a beer and listen to live music. The State of Colorado seized the business in the 1990s, after its one-time owner was arrested for dealing large quantities of marijuana. Now, in the vanguard state of legalized weed, Mishawaka is enjoying a renaissance, and the state collects the tax revenue.

Had I stayed for the summer, I could have had the opportunity to listen to both Ziggy Marley and Bruce Hornsby. I do not have time for either. As I make my way across the parking lot to observe a group of river-rafters heading down the Poudre, a young lady with a long dark braid and a butterfly tattoo on her left forearm stops her Subaru Forester and volunteers to drive me to Walden. Coloradans are proving to be the most hitchhiker-friendly crew yet.

Danica originally hails from Montana, but today she is on her way back from her grandfather's funeral in Cincinnati. Danica is hungry to get back to the mountains, back to her job with the Forest Service in Walden, ninety-two miles up the road and two thousand feet closer to heaven. She finds city life taxing. Even driving through the relatively mellow Fort Collins was wearing, and she was ready to get back to mountain peace and quiet.

The Poudre River Highway is the prettiest road I have ever ridden. With the river roaring east, always in sight just a few yards from the side window of the Forester, it gives me the feeling of racing westward, up the mountain, hugging the curves of bending two-lane blacktop. Danica is the perfect tour guide, and she narrates as we make our way through feathery groves of aspen in the Rawah Wilderness.

We can see snow on the mountaintops at ten thousand feet or more. Mule deer and elk graze near the road. We stop at the Joe Wright Reservoir, up at the tree line, just to look around. I learn about a hairy sunflower she calls The Old Man of the Mountain.

Scars are still visible from two drought-fueled fires that tore through the canyon in the spring of 2012. The Hewlett fire started when James Weber, a mental health counselor at Colorado State, tipped over his camp stove one day in early May. Weber made his way into town to sound the alarm, but by suppertime, the blaze had gobbled up two hundred-eighty acres of Forest Service land.

In a week, it would consume seventy-six-hundred acres and give work to four hundred firefighters. So light is the human footprint in the Gorge, that no lives were lost and not a single building burned. By Memorial Day, river rafters were again making their way down the Poudre, and that Sunday, a scheduled Mishawaka concert by the rock band, Toad the Wet Sprocket, proceeded as planned. James Weber paid a fine totaling three hundred, twenty-five dollars for failing to secure a permit before he lit his cook stove. The fire damage was estimated at nearly three million dollars.

Residents of the Gorge barely had time to catch their breath before a much more consequential fire erupted. The High Park Fire in early June consumed over eighty-seven thousand acres, burned down two hundred and fifty-nine homes, and killed one human, a sixty- two-year-old woman who had defied two evacuation orders. The Rockies seem to take this kind of shit in stride.

Danica finds Colorado a bit busy for her Montana tastes. She is an only child whose best friends growing up were her St. Bernard and a very special grandmother who spent summers with her family near Flathead Lake. Her Bible, Danica tells me, was written by John Muir, and her favorite way to relax is to take a hike up to a place called Rainbow Lake.

She might be the only twenty-four-year-old I know, who still uses a flip phone. She plans to ink her arms and shoulders with wildflowers and squid. Danica has a dream of working one day in South America, and I have no doubt she's gonna make that a plan. She is a keeper.

She sees bison a lot, but not mountain bison. They've gone extinct around here, she tells me.

There's elk and mountain goat, and relatively few humans, which is how Danica likes it. The number of plant species has also been dropping as the climate changes. She voices her concerns about the planet the way you might sound if you were talking about a sick relative. She listens avidly to Vice News and tries to absorb as much of the woods as her time allows.

The air is thinner and the trees sparser by the time we get to Walden, a town, according to Danica, "with one movie theater, one good pizza shop, and one bad pizza shop." It is also the self-proclaimed moose-watching capital of the world.

We have left the Poudre Canyon behind. Danica pulls the Subaru to the roadside near the good pizza shop. She goes off to her Forest Service barracks, and I set up on the western edge of town near a cemetery, where Route 14 continues up and on toward higher ground. From this spot, it feels like you can see forever—Wyoming to the north, Utah to the west, Breckinridge to the south.

The road west from Walden is one continuous climb.

The wind blows hard across the plain. Hardworking men and women in pickup trucks pass by, waving friendlily. They do not stop, nor do they seem surprised to see me there.

Ron picks me up in the middle of the afternoon, a few hours after Danica left me. Another pickup truck, another laborer. He is an electrical engineer, wiring a new resort in Wyoming. He describes it as a playground for the ultra-rich. Ron has mixed feelings.

It's nice work and it pays well, but it's all for the pleasure of people with what seems to him like ridiculous money. Ron would rather deploy his talents in something other than entertaining already-pampered elites. He'd rather we invest our money in other things, like education.

Which leads the conversation to politics. "I can't stand Trump," he volunteers. "These tax cuts for the rich," he says, "just put a burden on my kids." He roams far and wide, working hard, "determined that my kids won't be buried in debt."

It's the kids more than the politicians that are on Ron's mind. Tonight, he is heading back home, driving four hours across the mountain range to handle an errand for one of his two daughters. The girl was stuck in New York City when she realized that she needed some paperwork before heading to Europe for a semester abroad. Being a good Dad, Ron is spending his evening off, and will spend tomorrow's pre-dawn hours, on a four-hundred-mile round-trip to retrieve the papers and send them to her.

Our conversation meanders between family and the state of the world. Ron points to storm clouds to the north. He watches to see if they start to spin. Tornadoes at this altitude, he tells me, were unheard of a few years back. Now they come through regularly. He gets worked up again, this time railing against climate change deniers. "If you don't think the climate is changing and that we are what's causing it, you're just uninformed."

At the junction coming up, he is going to turn south and let me continue west toward Steamboat. It is not until that moment, when we know that our time together is coming to an end, that the conversation gets personal. He mentions his wife, Kathy, and asks me how long I've been married. We talk about marriage and how sweet lasting love can feel at our age. Ron nods and then shakes his head and whispers something about how quickly that can change. He tells me the story of his wife, Kathy.

I brace myself for a love story gone bad, something to explain the somber tone in his voice. I guessed wrong.

He loved Kathy until the day she died. She was fifty-seven years old and went in for surgery on her ankle. She came home that same night and died in her sleep. Ron woke up next to her and found she was gone.

This all happened less than two months ago. Just like that, he lost the love of his life and became the single dad to two college-age girls. And here he is, driving what amounts to a full shift in order to assist one of them. I have no doubt that he would have driven to New York and back for that girl, if such was required. And yet, on this errand, with a grieving heart, he stopped to pick up a stranger. Out of habit? Looking for company? Or just someone with whom to share the burden?

This devastating news tumbles out as we approach a roadblock. A state trooper waves us over and informs Ron that the road south is closed. Something about a wrecked truck and a brushfire. "Looks like I'll be going through Steamboat after all," says Ron. His misfortune is my good luck, but he doesn't seem upset. Distance is different out West.

As we start to pull away, the trooper's radio crackles and he raises his hand to stop us again.

Just like that, my luck turns again. The road south is clear, and Ron is taking it. He can save about an hour and, of course, I am happy for him. I just want another minute to give my condolences about Kathy. I can't imagine what it will be like to go home to that house.

I want to say something that will matter, try to tell him about Caroline, tell him that I know in some way what he is carrying in his heart. But there is a cop, and a couple of cars coming up behind us, and the urge to keep traffic moving, for what reason I can't say, so we shake hands like it's any other ride on any other day. I say goodbye and I wish him well.

I am about to trudge off into a mountain, facing sunset, hauling a backpack into uncertain terrain. My burden is light when I think about what Ron is facing.

On impulse, I ask the officer, "Why don't you take me to Steamboat?"

To my great surprise, Officer Stevens-Mejia of the Colorado State Patrol says okay. I stand by the side of the road, feeling lucky again as I wait for him to dismantle the roadblock, kick over the stumps of his emergency flares, and place the little orange cones in the trunk.

Then he asks for my license and runs a check for warrants. I think this is the third such check in my two-weeks-plus on the road, and so far all traces of my nefarious past appear to have been scrubbed from the official record, because the pleasant and chatty Officer Stevens-Mejia politely returns my license and pronounces my record clean.

Noting my New York driver's license, the young officer tells me he has family in New York State and has fond memories of summers spent at a camp in the Catskills.

"Now, in order to put you in the car, I have to search you and cuff you."

Really?

I look around at the fast-moving clouds and the aptly named

Rabbit Ears Pass towering above me. Calculating my chances of getting a ride in a vehicle that does not have protective glass between me and the front seat before the sun sets, I take the deal. Carefully, the officer places my backpack in the truck.

What follows is a ritual that you may have seen on TV. You may have experienced it in person. I remove a lot of objects from a lot of pockets, promise that I have no weapons, then remember the pocket-knife in my pack and fess up. I raise my arms, spread my legs and submit to a thorough search from head to toe. With that concluded, out come the cuffs. Officer Stevens- Mejia puts the cuffs on both wrists—in front, which is a lot easier—and places his left hand on top of my head, guiding me into the backseat. He leans over, buckles me in, and away we go.

Then he asks what type of music I like. He inquires if the AC is comfortable. The temperature is fine; he has no Springsteen. This is feeling a little weird.

The cuffs seem a bit excessive, not only to me, but to my friend Phil, a state trooper back in New York, to whom I later relay the story. "He cuffed you for a courtesy ride?" Phil is astonished.

But cuff me, the Colorado officer does. We start the climb up to Rabbit Ears. Now we are at ninety-eight hundred feet. I am beginning to think about what dinner options await me in Steamboat Springs. It's been a long time since I've eaten. They say that Steamboat is a pretty little town, a year-round resort with skiing late into the spring and paddling all summer and fall. My son Robert has told me about the mineral hot springs nearby at a place called Strawberry Park.

We cross the Continental Divide. From this exact point, every drop of rain that falls to the east rolls toward the Platte River and into the Missouri, which rolls on down to the Mississippi and ultimately the Gulf of Mexico and the Atlantic. A drop landing west of this spot would make its way to the Colorado River and on to the Pacific. At least it used to. The waters of the Colorado are now all consumed by farms and cities in the desert between the mountains and the coast. I wonder who is in charge of figuring out the exact location of the Divide.

I try to live in the moment and not get ahead of myself. This is especially important in the hitching life, where any hint of promises kept, or normal timelines respected, is an invitation to frustration. You just never know what's around the next bend.

We drive barely five minutes straight up the mountain, and the patrol car pulls over. The officer steps out. We are on a tiny parking spot off the northern side of the road, a patch of pavement barely big enough for two cars. It's just a wide spot in the road near the line separating Grand County from Routt County.

Officer Stevens-Mejia comes around to my side and opens the door. He loosens the cuffs and helps me out of the car, indicating, unconvincingly, that he thinks there might be a truck stop three miles up the road. As I stand up, I can still see the twin peaks of Rabbit Ears, the largest item in view, just to the north.

I thank the officer, and he gives me a card with a number to call if I get in any trouble. He then asks me to call the number on the card to give him a review. This is like Yelp for law enforcement. I take the card, but never make the call, not sure how I would grade him on a scale of one to ten.

What accounted for his sudden change of heart? Did he just get a text from his girlfriend, saying she'd gotten home early from the Walmart? Or maybe he remembered the part in his training where they said never ever take a hitchhiker across county lines.

It doesn't matter. We part ways, I hoist my pack and start walking west. It is a gorgeous setting, just perfect—if you happen to be a snow leopard.

Beneath the trees, a good foot or two of snowpack remains in places where the spring sunshine has yet to penetrate. Peaks covered in snow frame the landscape. There is no truck stop. There is nothing here but elk and moose, clouds, a few remaining hours of daylight, and me.

Uncuffed, deep in the mountains of one of the whitest states in the West, I have to ask myself the question that anyone with a web browser and a heartbeat must be thinking in this summer of 2018. I wonder how this experience would have gone, how I would feel right now, and where I would be spending the night, if I were a black man?

I have a good bit of time to think about that. I walk for an hour or more, worrying if the sun will last, or if I can handle the three-hour hike to Steamboat. I put one foot in front of the other, leaning into the hill.

Along comes Nazz. A white Camry stops. The passenger door swings open.

"I don't feel well."

Those are her first words.

"Do you want me to drive?"

"No, just get in."

And I did.

Nazz is her nickname—her given name is Nancy. She lives by herself in the mountains outside Walden. A few months ago, doctors removed her appendix. It is hurting today. Fearful it might be an abscess or worse, she made an appointment at a clinic in Steamboat for tomorrow morning. She holds her stomach with her right hand and drives with her left. She isn't sure it will hold until the morning.

Maybe I should drive you to the ER?

She isn't sure. Up and down the mountains, she narrates the contours of her discomfort.

We talk about the mountains. She's sixty-nine years old and lives alone. She isn't sure who would come if she took ill. The little clinic in Walden can't treat anything serious. But Nazz doesn't want to miss school tomorrow. It is supposed to be her last day on the job. After decades in the classroom, she doesn't want to miss the last day of classes.

She had weighed that against the chances of dying alone in her cabin. Instead of calling the ambulance, she started up the Camry, drove across the Rockies, and picked up a hitchhiker on a stretch of highway so empty and so beautiful it might as well have been on the moon. A few miles from Steamboat, (never did see a truck stop) she allows that maybe she's feeling a bit better.

I have always had a turbulent relationship with the concept of karma, or its pop-Christianity sibling, the notion that there is a powerful God, who provides everything we need. Whether they come from the East or the West, such notions seem to imply that we can't handle ourselves in this world without a magical voodoo doctor or a flying spaghetti monster. Or that somehow, when things go south, we get what we deserve.

On this mountain, I knew exactly what I needed—a ride to Steamboat and a place to sleep. Nazz needed someone to settle her down in the face of pain and a surging fear of what might be going wrong inside her gut. In a larger sense, I needed a lot of things. I needed Caroline to breathe and for her parents' tears to cease. I needed my country to stop shouting long enough to see the harm we were doing to the world around us. Nazz talked a lot about her son. It seemed that she needed to know that he loved her.

We found each other out there on the road just west of Rabbit Ears. I don't think it was karma, the result of some kind gesture I chose to make in my past. I don't think it was God putting Nazz in my path, the way Ricardo believed that Jesus had told him to stop for me back in Ohio. I think it was Nazz who made that choice because she was feeling vulnerable and wasn't afraid of that feeling. And I realized that I was out there for much the same reason.

I live on a vulnerable planet, in a vulnerable country, in a vulnerable family, all of us faced with choices—and in a culture that tells us, day and night, in person, online, and on film and TV, to shut that vulnerable part down and put on a brave front for the world.

Nazz chooses, in an exposed and powerless moment, to expose herself even further. I am doing the same. In that predisposition, find a kinship.

I think about the trooper who had left me at Rabbit Ears. He had all the power. He had his gun, his car, his radio, his shield, all his blessed procedures to protect himself. He even had handcuffs to deploy on a harmless guy old enough to be an AARP member. He had the power to drop me off where he chose, which wasn't a great spot.

Nazz had nothing. She had only her fear, her pain. And her freedom. She was hurting.

On the other side of the mountain, barreling toward Breckenridge, my earlier ride, Ron, is trying to salve his open wounds by doing a kindness to his college-bound daughter and, by some strange roadside coincidence, to me. He knows, Ron and Nazz both know, by some instinct that there is something to be gained, something possibly salvific in taking a chance, in stopping for a stranger.

Ron found someone to talk with, Nazz found company to reassure her that she would make it across that mountain pass alive. Both found something more. They found in themselves what they were hoping for, a reassurance that despite all the calamity and pain that rakes through our lives, with a planet in peril and a madman at the helm of a great power, we can still find one another along the way.

I had found the road. It still exists. Wherever that human instinct prevails, I think with satisfaction, the road lives. Reassuring.

By the time we reach the edge of Steamboat, Nazz tells me she doesn't think she needs to go to the ER. She mentions an inexpensive hotel on the edge of town. I offer to crash there. If the pain worsens in the night, she can knock on my door, and I'll take her to the hospital.

Nazz settles into her room at the Steamboat Hotel. I take the room next to hers, drop my pack on the bed, and open the window to listen to the rocky roar of the Yampa River. The Yampa runs right through Steamboat. Its current provides the warm weather yin that complements the snowy yang of winter to make this mountain town a year-round playground.

Nazz calls to meet me in the lobby. Still feeling okay. We ride in her car, going west along the river in search of a cup of tea, down the main road into downtown. In the heart of Steamboat Springs, we find Chris waiting tables at Johnny B Good's Diner.

We are the only ones in the place. I immediately like Chris. He looks like a hundred other skater boys we saw while driving through town, a little disheveled, supremely confident in his looks, and instinctively casual. I order a burger. He suggests that I try a side of their special bacon broccoli slaw. It is a very good idea.

He hangs around our table, and as I dig into my burger and Nazz sips her tea, something about Chris makes me want to know more. I ask what he is doing in Steamboat.

"Keeping a promise."

I look up from my burger.

Chris continues. "I've got a niece here. Her name is Unique Rose."

What a great name for a little girl. When Chris was twenty-one years old, he was lying in a hospital bed and most adults, including his doctors, thought he was dying of lymphoma. One hospital had given up on him. A friend had dragged him to another facility in Iowa. Doctors there gave him a thirty-percent chance.

Unique Rose came to visit Chris in the hospital. Her mother, Chris's twin sister, brought her to see her uncle. The adults in the room were probably thinking it might be goodbye.

Unique Rose was about four years old. Her eyes were level with Chris's face, lying in the bed. "Uncle Chris," she asked, "when you get better, will you come live with us in Steamboat?"

He didn't expect to live to fulfill it, but Chris made a promise to her that day. "Yes, Unique Rose, I will come live with you."

Now he's keeping that promise, serving broccoli slaw and burgers, enjoying a life he never expected to have. He beat cancer, left college six credits short of a degree, and came to live with a little girl, the only person he knew that believed for certain he wasn't going to die.

By the time we leave, Nazz is giving him a long hug, like only a mother can give.

Chris could have been just the guy who introduced me to bacon broccoli slaw. Now, he is Unique Rose's uncle, and I am his friend. He is part of my tribe, a tribe that I think is bigger than most of us imagine, the shifting population of "shut-down strangers" that Springsteen sang about in the seventies. And still sings about today.

Whether we know it or not, we're all on the same road, riding to the same sea, washing something we can't name off our hands. We're all on the road sometime. If we let ourselves take the chance. Nazz and Chris made this a special day of travel. Officer Stevens-Mejia, too.

America presents itself to the world the way we present ourselves to strangers, tough and indifferent. But inside, we have a vulnerable core, being a nation based on ideas and struggles, not blood lines, on a hope more than certainty.

Which doesn't mean we don't crave the scent of certainty. We get it where we can find it, sometimes from triumph, sometimes from false prophets, sometimes from our songs and poems, and in rare moments, from the struggle to be true to our ideals. Even when standing by the side of the road seems futile and boring, I have to believe it is valuable to nurture the impulse to be vulnerable, to be open to what comes next. Fear is always on the edge of our consciousness. The gold is in what we do when dread tries to overwhelm our vision.

This American moment is being defined as a struggle over what to do with our most vulnerable people. Eject them, wall them off, objectify them, or slow down, stop, listen, and take them, maybe even drive them, an extra mile?

The sturdiest and safest people on Earth are being convinced that we are the most put-upon, the downtrodden. We remain spectacularly generous. In town after town across the country, the one thing I see without fail is posters for Barbecues and Potlucks, community events to raise money for neighbors afflicted by illness or other misfortunes. And we all turn out. We turn out for the ones we know, the ones we can relate to. That's a good thing.

But the tribe out on the road takes generosity a step beyond. My tribe out on the road feels a certain urgency for reaching out to those who are different, those who are unknown. Those strangers. I find something refreshing in that. In Nazz, in Ron, and in Chris.

Colorado. You keep me going.

# 14

## Steamboat Waters to Dusty Craig

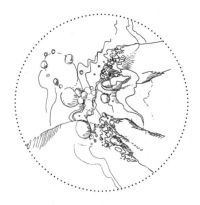

I wake up rested in my room at the Steamboat Hotel. My first thought is of Nazz. I knock on her door. No response. I ask the woman at the front desk, a beautiful Jamaican lady. She hasn't seen her. I go out to the parking lot and see Nazz's car is gone.

Whether she went home or to the hospital, she left early and alone. I feel sad. A little bit abandoned. And worried for her.

I walk out in the direction of Johnny B Good's. Steamboat Springs has a free bus that takes you all over town. I hop on and get a tour of the village. Sitting next to me is a young man from El Salvador, about to start his first day of work at a resort. Along the river, men are fly fishing and practicing kayaking against the current, making their way up and down the Yampa.

My new friend Chris isn't working the morning shift at the diner, but I meet Hannah, an ebullient girl in camo, who recommends the Reuben Omelet, a plate that may qualify as the best breakfast of the trip. She also tells me that she is planning to run a half marathon this weekend.

After breakfast, I am tempted to get going on the road west. Instead, I get a ride to Strawberry Park Hot Springs with a guy named Rob. Strawberry Park is a natural hot spring that people have been telling me about for years. Rob, a transplant from New Jersey, drops me in the parking lot, where young girls in batik skirts and long braided ponytails are getting stoned along with their rock-climber boyfriends.

Strawberry Park is the best fifteen bucks anyone can spend in the Rockies. It's a piece of heaven cut from stone. I can only imagine what it is like under the stars. Steaming hot water comes out of the mountain and runs down into a series of pools. A mountain stream runs by on one side, and you can jump from the steamy hot water to the cold river.

God, does it feel good to get that pack off and soak my bones for a couple of hours! There are only a few dozen people slipping in and out of the waters, or hiking the trails, barely making a sound. An occasional cloud drifts by.

And there is a moment, one brief special moment, with the stream from a slender waterfall splashing off my head and shoulders, when I look up at the mountains. No one can see me through this wall of water. I realize that I am crying, and smiling, my own tears merging with the steaming, magical mineral water coming out of the rock.

It is as if the water is giving me permission to let go of what I am holding in. I have a deep sense of Caroline being there with me in that pool. My granddaughter lived her entire life completely under water, in the perfect world of her mother's womb. I often think of her happy life there, swimming inside her mom with my son Daniel's strong arms around her and Jules.

This water washes over me and I think of Caroline, moving and swimming and sucking her thumb, the way we sometimes see babies doing on ultrasounds.

I never got to play with her. A thousand times, I imagined us playing. A thousand different ways. Swinging her high over my head. Pushing her on a swing, holding her on a bike. Hiking, climbing, rolling, laughing, and playing so many ways. I pictured her swimming a lot.

Strawberry Park was our chance to play together. We swam. I cried. I could hear her laughing as we played. The water tumbled over us. I don't know anyone here, and no one in my world knows where I am. I am invisible. It is the greatest freedom I have felt since the awful day that she died.

Most of the days and weeks after Caroline's death, Ellen and I had been there primarily as backup to the parents. Their grief was so enormous, unfathomable, and primary. I was so proud of them, and so pained for them. There was no room for my own tears. Today, for the first time, in the water, I have Caroline to myself. I can covet this freedom to feel the blend of my own longing and joy and pain all alone, and to feel it melt into the water pouring over me.

There will never be another Caroline. But we will live for her, even more than before, knowing how precious these breaths we take can be and how fleeting they are.

When I meet up with my ride, Rob, in the parking lot, he is playing Springsteen on his satellite radio. He had checked out my hitchhiker blog and read the story of the trooper asking me what kind of music I liked, but not having any Springsteen on tap.

Turns out, this Rob is not only from New Jersey, but born and raised in Flemington, just a few blocks from the home of the late Danny Federici, the E Street keyboard player. We make our way back to the highway, two Eastern boys humming "Hungry Heart" and "Thunder Road" high up in the Rockies.

An hour later, I hop into a white Nissan Sentra with a happy hobbit of a young man named Jamie. Another refugee from a family plagued by addiction.

Jamie fled to Steamboat, where he works as a snowboard instructor in the winter and a geology tour guide the rest of the year. He helps tourists understand the time before there were mountains here, when the Rockies were an ocean. "See all this," he says, pointing to the limestone cliffs on the roadside. "It's basically shells." Best geology lesson I ever had.

Jamie is a hitchhiker for the digital era. A few years ago, he hiked the Appalachian Trail from end to end, staying with virtual friends he had met through online gaming. His version of the road passes through games we had never imagined forty years ago.

Jamie takes me twenty-five miles, to the town of Hayden, where I soon meet Richard and Val. It is 3:27 in the afternoon, and eighty-one degrees. Richard is at least the third driver who turns around and pulls a U-turn so he can pick me up. He is transporting a woman named Val from an eye doctor appointment in Steamboat, back to her apartment in Craig. She has on those big sunglasses they give you when they dilate your pupils.

This is Richard's retirement job. He's driven a million miles, taking patients to the doctor and back, usually accompanied by Casey, a Chihuahua/Shih Tzu mix he happily spoils. Richard used to ride a Harley with a baby seat rigged up on the back, just for Casey.

He had to quit riding the bike after cancer surgery. He just doesn't have the strength in his legs to keep the 750 upright. This old truck he's driving is filling in while his new car is being repaired. Richard sheepishly explains how he blew up the electrical system on that one, after he rigged up a fan to the battery to keep little Casey cool in the Colorado summer. It's going to be a major repair bill, but he tells me the story anyway. He loves that dog like a grandbaby.

A few miles east of Craig, Richard points out the ranch where he was raised. There's a For Sale sign swinging from a post. Ranching is going south, coal mines are shutting down, and the coal-powered plant that defines the skyline of Craig, population of eight thousand and counting down, is slated to close in a few years.

Richard is one of the lucky ones. He has a pension that survives the coal mine that shut down fourteen years ago. His passenger, Val, is not so lucky. Skinny and sun-beaten, she smokes reservation cigarettes as we ride toward the sun.

Years back, New York State was debating whether to allow oil and gas companies to use hydrofracking technology to pull gas out of the Marcellus Shale, a formation not far south of Syracuse. Most of my environmentalist friends viewed this as seriously as a war crime. They viewed farmers and landowners who leased their land to the oil companies as fools or profiteers, or both.

Reporting on that story for our local newspaper, I met farm families so poor they couldn't pay their health insurance. Their kids had all moved away. The factories that once offered benefits and pensions were shuttered or replaced with sleazy operations that paid a fraction of a middle-class wage.

One couple I met used their royalty check from the gas company to pay for the husband's heart medicine—tens of thousands of dollars every year. These people knew fracking was a problem, but they couldn't get anyone in the state to answer the question: What are we going to do instead? Let his heart stop?

Fracking got banned. Those areas are still getting poorer. Doesn't have to be that way.

Val must have read my mind. "When they take away the coal," she says, "they take away your house. They take away your truck, then your kids." I can see why a woman in her situation might lend an ear when someone says "they" are now talking about taking away her gun.

We pull into Craig. Val lives in a second-floor apartment in a beat-up public housing project that once was a motel perched on the side of a divided Highway US-40, this city's faded Miracle Mile. The porches are filled with idle men and women leaning on railings made of painted 2x4s, watching traffic go by, smoking cigarettes. The parking lot looks like a junkyard. It isn't hard to see where a coal town like Craig is headed—more Val, less Richard, with each passing year.

Richard leaves me near the western edge of town, advising me not to take a ride unless it's going all the way to Vernal. There is no hospitable place in the desert for the next hundred and twenty miles.

Just as he drops me off at the Loaf 'N Jug gas station, a handsome young German couple, a man and a woman, scoop up their bags and hop into a minivan. I barely have time to say goodbye to Richard and Casey. I make a move in the direction of the van, but the driver signals that he is full—no room for me.

Cheryl Strayed wrote about hiking the Pacific Coast Trail in her book, *Wild*, later made into a movie with Reese Witherspoon. Strayed does a great job portraying the double-edged sword of gender and travel, describing the creepy guys she runs away from, and the good guys who pick her up to keep her safe. A threesome of happy-go-lucky trust fund boys christen her the "Queen of the PCT" because of how easily she gets favors from men. She accepts the title, and the risks.

The same applies to women and hitching. Women are in greater danger and are also more likely to get rides. I just watched a woman get picked up in a matter of minutes. In the moment, I took that as an encouraging sign. At least somebody still hitchhikes out here. I was very wrong. That spot on the edge of Craig became my home for the next two days.

The Loaf 'N Jug is the last place that cars, heading west into the desert, stop to load up on fuel, tobacco, or alcohol. A steady parade of cars and trucks, and trucks pulling trailers, make their way in and out of the lot.

A tractor-trailer pulls up just in front of me on my side of the road. The driver emerges and waves me off, semi-apologetic. He is just checking his tires before continuing west. Can't take the risk of picking up a rider. A white pickup pulls out of the Loaf 'N Jug and stops right next to me. White cowboy hat on his head and a can of beer in his hand, the driver asks where I'm headed.

"Vernal," I reply.

Two ranch hands in back, also drinking beer, laugh their asses off. The driver says he can take me to a spot fifteen miles up the road. I mention that I was advised not to get stuck in the middle of the desert because no one will stop for me out there. The driver agrees that this was good advice.

He has a different idea. "You looking for a job? We got work."

I have never worked as a ranch hand. "No, thanks." I tell them that I have a job.

The boys in the back of the white pickup find that hilarious.

"This is my vacation," I add, which pretty much ends my job interview.

The boss man offers me a piece of parting advice. Nodding toward my clever hashtag, he suggests, "What you need is a sign that says, 'I need a ride to Vernal.'" The chorus in back erupts like cartoon hyenas once more. Pleased to be able to provide entertainment for the desert ranch hands of northwest Colorado, I thank them all and walk back to my perch.

The cashier at the Loaf 'N Jug appears puzzled when I appear at the register a few minutes before six p.m., asking for a piece of cardboard and a Sharpie marker. She directs me to the dumpster out behind the gas station. "If you can find some cardboard there, come back in."

I go out back, lean inside the dumpster, and manage to extract a decent-size, brown cardboard box. The cashier looks surprised to see me again, but in between dexterously dispensing cigarettes, gas, beer, chips, and scratch-off tickets to customers, she hands me a black Sharpie marker, which I utilize to make my new sign.

No hashtag. Just "Vernal." It is a crappy sign.

The cashier takes the pen back, admonishing me to be careful.

My new sign holds about as much allure as the old one. Traffic heading west has to contend with sun in their eyes and a hill to climb. If they even notice me, it doesn't make much of a difference. I spend the next two hours listening to cars and trucks accelerate past me, and observing the heavy machinery going the other way, climbing back and forth on the serpentine switchbacks taking them to the coal-powered energy plant in the distance, to the south.

Every other vehicle coming in from the west, it seems, is heading to the plant. Cleaning, maintenance, deliveries—it is all about the coal.

A sensible person would call it a day. But we hitchhikers are not sensible people. A hitchhiker is like a drinker, or a gambler. We always want just one more. Just one more.

I had spotted the Hampton Inn across the road when I landed here, courtesy of Richard, hours ago. As I watch the sun drop into the desert, objectively speaking, a beautiful sight, it seems increasingly likely that this establishment will be my resting place for the night. But I won't give up. I keep telling myself that the next time the light turns green, someone will pull over and pick me up. Just one more.

This works for about ten cycles. Red. Orange Green. Red Orange Green. Red again. Still, no one stops. I realize I have to set myself some kind of limit, or I could end up standing here all night. Just ten more cycles, I promise to no one but myself, sounding like I'm pleading with a bartender.

Just as the light changes for the ninth time, a black SUV pulls over and stops. I run to the car, lean my pack against the back door, try to open the front door—and I hear a scream. The woman in the driver's seat looks up from her smartphone, sees my face and shrieks so loudly, they can probably hear her on the ranch out in the desert where I will not be working.

The frightened woman hits the gas, spinning my pack to the ground, and causing me to jump backwards to stay clear of her!

What in the name of Jesus? (This is not what I said.) Oh, the damned cell phone. This little spit of macadam is the last place anyone leaving Craig can get a decent signal on their phone. That's why she stopped. Not to pick me up, but to check text messages and email before heading out into the void beyond Verizon.

I feel like a man unjustly accused of a felony. I can still see the horror in her eyes. We did not have this problem in 1978. Verizon's service didn't suck. It didn't exist. Dusting myself off, I want to run after her to assure that I am not a child molester, or a rapist, merely a hitchhiker.

Realizing that chasing after a young woman's car in a frenzied state probably isn't a good look, I give up. She is gone. I am done for the day. In the last wisps of daylight, I walk toward the hotel, crossing over six lanes of traffic.

When you drive a car and you pull off at an exit, it takes no time at all to get to the gas station, or the Denny's, or the Econo Lodge. When you make that same trek on foot, you realize two things. One, it is farther than you think. Two, whoever designed these roads never thought anyone would be walking along them. It's dangerous.

It's just a dusty, cluttered, ugly path. Even taking a shortcut, I walk more than a mile to reach the Hampton Inn parking lot.

A lot of people ask me if I ever turn down a ride. Yes. I do. In Craig. Right now.

Just before I reach the inn, a semi stops to offer me a ride. The driver's name is Eduardo. He is friendly enough. He has an Eastern European accent. Eduardo is headed south, which is not a deal-breaker, but then he tells me that he has only four miles left to drive today. After that, he is maxed out. It sounds like a stranger is volunteering to drive me four miles into the high desert to spend the night with him in the cab of his semi.

It would be nice to save the eighty bucks, but my Spidey sense kicks in, and I turn him down. I give him a wristband and my thanks, but I decline the ride. Happy Trails, Eduardo, wherever you may be.

The next morning, over coffee in the breakfast room at the Hampton Inn, I meet Lyle Valora, courtesy of *The Craig Daily Press*, a paper which, in spite of its name, publishes thrice weekly. Mr. Valora is already dead, but a spunky obituary writer at *The Press* has brought him back to life in a most vivid manner.

*The Press* reminds me of why I love reading a dead-tree paper, as opposed to scrolling through a news website on my phone. Mr. Valora is the prime example. Do you remember the last time you clicked on the obits tab of a news site? Probably when someone you knew had passed away, and you wanted to know where the funeral was.

I don't know a soul in Craig and have not packed any clothes fit to wear to a wake, but that morning when I turn the page in *The Daily Press* and come face-to-face with Mr. Valora, a recently departed coal miner and heavy equipment operator from Hayden, my life feels enriched.

Mr. Valora, *The Press* informs me, badly injured an arm in a 1982 chainsaw accident. It put him out of work for ten years. He got cracking as an advocate for people with disabilities, even making a trip to Washington to advocate for passage of the Americans with Disabilities Act (ADA). Lyle Valora is quoted in the obit saying that he wanted to change the laws so that he could go back to work and support his family. When he was legally allowed, he did go back to work for the Colowyo Coal Company, retiring in 2013 with thirty years in the mine.

I know I'd be a poorer man if I had not spotted the smiling face of Mr. Valora as I sipped my morning coffee. May he rest in peace.

Another tidbit in *The Daily Press* catches my eye, a rather pedestrian but well-written piece about the county budget. Coal is key in Craig, and coal, you may have heard, is having a bit of a poor spell. Mostly because natural gas has become a cheaper source of energy, but also because people and the government have gotten tired of coal, the dirtiest of fossil fuels, fouling the air and warming the atmosphere.

Note that I am writing this after having (spoiler alert) gotten out of Craig at long last, because I did not want to offend the good people of Craig, not one of whom would have a bad word to say about the eleven local coal mines that pay more than twenty dollars per hour, double the minimum wage that they're likely to be offered when the mines close, and they go hunting for work in a tourist trap in Steamboat Springs.

Coal money funds everything in Craig—including the sole museum in town, which is on the chopping block if they can't find another way to keep the lights on.

Though it is hard to imagine today, coal mining had its moment at the forefront of the progressive movement in the United States, a little more than a century ago. In 1913, the largely Greek immigrant miners working the Rockefeller-owned Ludlow mine in southern Colorado, got fed up at the wages and working conditions, organized and struck, sparking a nearly two-year- long battle known as the Coal Field War. The war in the coalfields was an important part of labor movement history, an effort that led to the establishment of the eight-hour working day. It inspired a gruesome ballad by Woody Guthrie, entitled "The Ludlow Massacre."

Once I part ways with the Craig newspaper and tear myself away from the all-you-can-eat breakfast buffet, I once again confront the reality that no one in Craig seems to want to pick me up. Spend enough hours in one spot on the roadside, and you start to feel a need to shake things up a little. You can get superstitious, like a gambler who fingers a button on his sports jacket, or a ballplayer who circles the plate before stepping into the batter's box.

You start to glorify rituals. Posture. Positioning. The angle of the hat. Am I squinting? Why do they keep driving right past me? If I can just figure out what's in the mind of each of those drivers passing by, maybe I can alter my routine and, magically, the next car will stop. And if that works, I tell myself, I can get out of Craig and move on westward.

Then you run out of tricks. In the face of too much stoic, tinted-window rejection, you run out of patience. It's been a long morning already, and after two cars stop on the roadside to check their phones, fooling me into thinking they are stopping for me, I decide that it is time for a complete makeover.

I check my maps. I text Robert, my Colorado son, for his thoughts. The plan had been to keep hitching west on Highway 40 and to stay off the Interstate. The town of Creston, Wyoming, on I- 80 is less than a hundred miles north. Busy I-70 sits just an hour and change to the south. I decide to find a road headed north into Wyoming to catch I-80

West to Salt Lake City. That road is State Route 13. Lucky number? What was I thinking?

With no idea what Route 13 looks like, or how friendly Creston, Wyoming, might be to hitchhikers, it still seems like a better idea than begging for rides on the western edge of Craig, Colorado.

Walking a total of eight miles through Craig, I pass more signs for garage sales than I have seen in my entire life. There are also some interesting campaign signs posted by candidates running for County Coroner. This makes me curious. Who runs for County Coroner? Why is that an elected office?

Well, it turns out that the current coroner is also a local chiropractor. He is being challenged in the Republican primary by his assistant, who is also a local funeral director. There is a Democratic candidate, but no one seems to think he has a chance. It turns out they are right. The major issue in the campaign concerns the rising cost of transporting corpses.

The Pacific Ocean remains a stubborn one thousand, twenty-one miles away. I am not making a lot of progress getting out of Craig. The dust, the heat, the heartbreak of cars stopping and pulling away, even the screaming woman who drove away into the desert to get away from me—it is all worth it, just for the chance to converse with Bill Mackin.

Bill looks old enough to have been a witness to the Coal Field War. I meet him after crossing Yampa Avenue on my way north toward the edge of town, in search of a ride to Wyoming. The Museum of Northwest Colorado is open. I walk in, and Bill is the only one there.

He has trouble hearing. He breathes through a cannula on his nose which runs to an oxygen tank, strapped across his chest. But none of that bothers Bill. It's his memory that bothers him, he confides to me, just moments after he greets me. "I've got Alzheimer's," says Bill. "I'm kinda the local historian. A historian without a memory," says Bill, "ain't worth much."

By the time I leave Bill, an hour and a half later, he has proved his introductory statement false. He may feel that he's slipping, but his memories of an amazing life on the high plains are crisp and fascinating. Bill grew up in this area, traveling all over the West, trading guns and horses, both of which he considered enjoyable hobbies. He is a hunter, and the museum walls are lined with both the weapons he used to hunt, as well as dozens of stuffed mule deer, mountain lions, and other prey.

Somehow along the way, he ended up in Salt Lake City, where it is hard to find liquor, but Bill proved to be skilled at hunting this as well. After decades of heavy drinking, he took the first of twelve steps, turned his life around, and became one of the first substance abuse counselors in the State of Utah. Bill eventually became a psychologist, and made a career in mental health and alcoholism treatment that lasted thirty years.

I've never managed to attain the status of a full alcoholic, though I've been associated with enough "friends of Bill" that I feel like, if Alcoholics Anonymous had a farm team, I might be allowed to pitch in relief or at least ride the bench. Bill Mackin's story moves me to tell him the story of my own father, a friend of AA founder, Bill W., for decades, and a recovered alcoholic who also dealt with Alzheimer's in his final years.

The hitchhiker and the old horse trader share an embrace, and we each wipe a tear before I depart.

I leave Bill at the museum, thinking that if I had walked all the way across the country just to spend an afternoon with him, it would have been completely worthwhile. And he didn't even give me a ride.

*"I have so many thoughts,*
*not enough words."*

*– Jeff*

# 15

## Leaving Salt Lake and Desert Fever

On August 2, 1978, Joe and I left Grand Teton National Park, headed south toward Salt Lake City. With the help of four rides, including a short hop in the back of a pickup driven by a man named Dud Agree, we made it as far south as Ogden, Utah, on Interstate 15. Under a pine tree, near a football field, we spent our first night of that summer sleeping by the side of the road. All these years later, Joe and I still dissolve into a six-pack-or-more kind of laughing fit with the simple mention of the two words, "Dud Agree."

That is a tough name to forget (even tougher to google).

The next morning, we caught a five-mile ride in a pickup driven by Calvin, then rode about ten miles in a Mustang with a driver too drunk to give us his name, and finally were delivered to a Denny's

Restaurant on the edge of Salt Lake by Randy, a handsome blond man driving a VW bus.

The Denny's hostess marched us—backpacks, guitar, and all—past a contingent of police officers seated at the counter. Fortunately, the way we smelled was not a crime in the state of Utah, though it probably should have been considered a public health violation. After six days in the mountains, we had no memories involving soap and warm water, or for that matter, the sensation of being indoors. When we sat down, the Naugahyde cover on those hideous, two-toned Denny's booth seats felt like a warm embrace.

Then things got strange. As we devoured our Grand Slam breakfasts, walkie talkies went off one by one, cops stepped out in a hurry, and soon the counter was deserted. Worried-looking waitresses looked at one another as they cleared a line of plates and half-empty coffee mugs.

Cops leaving their coffee to get cold means something serious is afoot. We feared for the safety of President Carter. When you grow up in the sixties, you always think like that.

Interstate 80 now runs essentially from the George Washington Bridge to the Golden Gate, but when Joe and I came through, they were still working on the last stretch, right here at the edge of Salt Lake City. As we walked out of the Denny's, cars were bumping along an unpaved detour. One of those cars, a Chevy Caprice with a wooden canoe on the roof, stopped right in front of us.

A bearded hippie named Jeff opened the door and invited us in. By prior arrangement, it was Joe's turn to ride shotgun. I crammed in the back with Jeff's dog, an old yellow Lab, who we later learned had long ago lost her hearing. So we never verified if the dog's name was "Dog," or "God." Jeff was a classic hippie stoner, blissfully making a pilgrimage from Steamboat Springs to the Bay Area. On this day, he was a messenger of doom.

"Some crazy lady is throwing her kids out of a hotel window."

Over Jeff's car radio we learned what had caused the dramatic exodus of law enforcement from the Denny's. Rachel David, the wife of a cult leader, had marched her seven children onto the eleventh floor balcony of the International Dunes Inn, and was in the process of tossing them, one by one, over the edge—in her mind, freeing them from the bonds of earthly suffering to join their Daddy in heaven.

The earthly daddy, Immanuel David, had just done himself in with carbon monoxide as an FBI investigation of his crooked finances closed in on him. On that balcony, Rachel stacked chairs up so the littlest ones could reach the railing. Story is, they went willingly.

It would be wrong to judge the entire state of Utah based on this small sample, and important to note that Immanuel David was not a Mormon. The Church of Latter-Day Saints had had the good sense, years earlier, to excommunicate the sword-brandishing, three-hundred-pound man with a ponytail, when he first began to declare himself the Creator, the Messiah, and the Holy Ghost.

His wife and children never escaped his thrall, so much so that the one daughter, who miraculously survived the fall from the balcony, still tells guests at her assisted living facility that she believes that her father, the Savior, will soon return to Earth in all his glory.

But I digress. The Salt Lake City that welcomes me in the summer of 2018 is a very different place. I crash at the home of my old friend, a fellow Syracuse writer named Tom Kahley, who shows me around a very cosmopolitan downtown scene.

In the morning, Tom suggests that I take the casino bus to Wendover, a border town, for about ten dollars. I find my way to the bus depot, but just can't bring myself to buy the ticket. I start walking in the still cool of morning, toward the ramp leading to I-80 West.

And then I see the Denny's, the same Denny's where Joe and I had settled into those booths forty years ago. I stand in front and look toward downtown, toward the newly renovated Shilo Inn, the successor to the fateful International Dunes. It is the same place. That can only mean one thing—it is time for another Grand Slam breakfast.

Lots has changed in the forty years since Joe and I caught that ride with Jeff, the hippie with the deaf dog. Most of the Denny's staff are speaking Spanish to one another. The Grand Slam has morphed, in the manner of Ritz Crackers, Oreos, and Budweiser, into multiple, varied Grand Slams. It used to be you ordered a Grand Slam, and they asked you how you wanted your eggs. It was two pancakes, two eggs, two sausage links, and two strips of bacon shut up and eat.

Today you can order a Lumberjack Slam, an All-American Slam, a Belgian Waffle Slam, or the hilariously titled "Fitness Slam," as in "I think I'll skip the gym and go over to Denny's to work on my fitness." Customizing your own slam is also an option, this being the era of customized everything, thank you Starbucks and Steve Jobs. I just order the Grand Slam. It is good.

After finishing up, I post an image of the Denny's to Instagram, walk three blocks past an encampment where homeless men are still waking up, and set myself up on the I-80 westbound ramp. Just a few miles away, airplanes lift off from the Salt Lake International Airport. Traffic chugs by on the highway.

I barely have a minute to settle in, when a nice Ford pickup stops. It even backs up toward me. I throw my pack in the backseat, climb in the front, and introduce myself.

"I'm Ed."

"Hi, I'm Jeff." Another Jeff outside the same Denny's. What an insane coincidence.

This Jeff tells me that he is out shopping for cabinets at Home Depot. Instead, he takes me for a two-hour ride all the way to the Nevada border, another kind person taking me far out of his way. This clean-cut, handsome Jeff from 2018 is a far cry from hippie-Jeff of 1978, but they both take me for a hell of a ride.

It is not, in my experience, difficult to maintain a steady course on a four-lane interstate highway. For this Jeff, it presents a challenge. He chats happily as he drives his new, beautiful four-door pickup truck, mostly in the left-hand lane, at speeds approaching ninety miles per hour, not uncommon out on the salt flats. But on at least two occasions, Jeff just drives right off the exit. The exit ramps are well marked, yet Jeff seems puzzled to find himself no longer on the roadway.

He keeps the truck under control, turns right, then left, then left again, meandering through subdivisions and desert back roads for ten or twenty minutes. His mind wanders in the same way. It makes me a little uneasy.

Jeff is certain about what he knows. He knows that there is a tunnel underground between Salt Lake and San Francisco, filled with water. He knows that the government lowered submarines into the tunnel years back. Government mining operations caused the tunnel to collapse, precipitating a drought that lasts till the present moment. We are driving through so much desert that you might start to empathize with the desire to believe such things.

Jeff also knows that the Earth has a hollow cylinder running through it, from pole to pole, like the cardboard center of a roll of paper towels. It is called Center Earth. Air Force planes fly in and out of Center Earth, and chemicals released from this space, which is off-limits and not even accessible to the President, these chemicals emerge at the North Pole and create the spectacular phenomenon that we, in our blissful ignorance, refer to as the Northern Lights.

Hitler, Jeff tells me, knew about Center Earth, as do modern elites, who meet regularly in Antarctica, where—and they do not want any of us to know this—they have discovered pyramids. Also, skeletons of humans ranging from eight to thirty-six feet tall.

To run into Jeff on the street, or the highway, you would not suspect that he harbors any unorthodox thoughts. He looks healthy and neat, like he is successful at something, and that he goes to the gym a lot. Then he starts talking. He's trying to decide whether to move to Costa Rica and open a treetop bed-and-breakfast, or move to Tennessee, where he's got his eyes on a hundred-and-fifty-acre farm with the perfect conditions for growing bamboo.

He owns dirt bikes and a paraglider, and on this day, at around five in the afternoon, he is driving me west to the edge of the Utah desert and trying to decide, when he gets home, where he is going to take the family camping in his RV, because it is Saturday.

We are still heading west, and I am not convinced that any of this is true, or even that Jeff has a wife, or children, or a house. I'm not even sure if this is his truck and that his name is Jeff.

That happens once in a while. In the second week of our 1978 trip, Joe and I spent a day hopping in and out of the back of pickup trucks, progressing slowly southwest through Ontario. Finally, we crossed back over from Windsor, Canada, into Detroit. It was dark by the time we made our way to the Greyhound station. We had just spread out and set ourselves up to spend the night sleeping on the floor beneath a bench, when we were approached by Benji, a fast-talking character in a brown furry jacket.

Benji asked where we were going. Not waiting for an answer, he said he had run out of gas and offered us a ride to Jackson, Michigan, in exchange for gas money.

Back then, you could fill a tank for ten dollars. Joe and I caucused, decided to take the risk, and offered Benji four bucks.

He hesitated.

So did we.

The sticky floor of the dingy Detroit bus station didn't seem that uninviting, compared to a ride into the darkness with a hustler. Benji took the deal. Joe and I exchanged one last questioning glance, shrugged and shouldered our packs. I grabbed the guitar, and we followed Benji to the exit door.

Outside was a brand-new Lincoln Continental. Not the vehicle you expect a guy with no gas money to be driving. Benji climbed into the front, where his pal Ronny was behind the wheel. They drove us off into the night, after about ten minutes spent figuring out how to turn on the headlights. Joe extracted his trusty roadmap from a zipped-up side pocket, and gave Benji and Ronny directions to exit Greater Detroit.

Joe and I had more than enough reason to suspect that the car we were riding in was stolen. When we drove into a downpour, and neither

Benji nor Ronny were able to find the windshield wipers, Joe reached from the backseat and switched them on just in time to avoid hitting the guardrails.

Yes, sometimes even car thieves pick up hitchhikers. Benji and Ronny eventually dropped us off at a campground near Jackson and went on their way.

In the Utah desert, in 2018, I don't get a chance to find out if Jeff knows how to operate the wipers in his truck. My guess is that he did not steal the vehicle, but his rambling conversation makes it evident that something very odd is going on in his mind. I find it plausible that he has two dogs, and one may be a chiweenie. The chances that the other is a hermaphrodite French Bulldog—your guess is as good as mine.

To my great relief, Jeff is astute enough to find the interstate again, and kind enough to drive me all the way across Utah to the border town of Wendover. The Mormon side of Wendover has nary a tavern in sight, but the Nevada half offers visitors the opportunity to indulge in at least seven sins.

Even with Jeff's peculiarities on display, I cannot help but like him. He is guileless, friendly, and unimposing. He does not try to foist his views of the world on me. He just shares openly and effortlessly the great thoughts he has amassed during his forty-six years on Earth—at least some of those years, he mentions in passing, spent "locked up."

"I have so many thoughts, not enough words," says Jeff. "I want to write a book."

Over a lifetime of listening, I have come to realize that there are many people who think that this is the purpose of books, to help people with too many thoughts and not enough words get them out of their heads. Ricardo, the trucker who gave me the lift through Ohio to Kentucky, expressed the same yearning. He wanted me to come to Florida to help him write it all down.

Jeff did have one characteristic in common with Ricardo, and with many great authors—an eye for detail and description. The precision of his delusions intrigues me. The giants found in Center Earth are not just gigantic—they measure between eight and thirty-six feet tall. The edifices under the Antarctic ice are not just buildings, they are pyramids. And his vision of his mountain in Tennessee, if it is a delusion, is decorated with, of all things, a bamboo plantation. (Appalachian bamboo, it turns out, might actually be a good investment.)

His regular source of information, Jeff later informs me, is Alex Jones, the radio talk jockey and the brains behind the InfoWars website. Alex is "one hundred percent freedom, one hundred percent Constitutional," Jeff tells me. "He tries to let us know the truth. He's awesome." And they are on a first name basis.

Alex Jones and I have very few shared thought patterns. Yet, when Jeff realizes that I am from Syracuse, his brain immediately punches up a name—Michael Rotondo.

My Syracuse pride groans quietly. Rotondo is an underdeveloped male in his early thirties, from just outside the city, who recently made international news after his parents were forced to take him to court to evict him from their basement. The judge quickly concluded that this cellar-dweller was too annoying even for kin to have to put up with, and gave young Michael the boot.

Rotondo promptly failed to make support payments of fifty-eight dollars per month to feed the eight-year-old child he had inexplicably managed to sire. Court documents later revealed that he did continue to pay two thousand dollars a year for storage of his broken 1989 Camaro.

As a Syracusan, as a male—hell, as a human being—I am embarrassed to be having a conversation about this cretin. To add insult to insult, for some reason Alex Jones thought it a good idea to give this young deadbeat in a child support battle a microphone and three thousand dollars to tell his pathetic story.

It used to be that travelers from Syracuse were asked about basketball coach Jim Boeheim, our resident petulant male. Now those seem like the good old days, like when Bush the father was in charge.

Really, we do have some cool people in Syracuse. Come visit. You will love it. I promise.

Jeff suddenly seems to have all day ahead of him and is planning to wander Wendover in search of music. But it is time to say goodbye.

Jeff's casual manner, as he related his bizarre and incoherent stories, highlighted one of the changes that I've noticed in these past forty years—the gap between the country Jimmy Carter governed, and the one now tweeted upon by Donald Trump. Carter has said on occasion that when he ran for office, he always knew that there was a percentage of the population that was crazy—impervious to facts, to logic, or reason. He estimated that about three percent of the nation fell into this fringe category. You might include Rachel David, who threw her children off that hotel balcony in 1978, in their ranks.

Since the advent of cable news and social media, that cohort has grown to about twenty percent—a big difference. With Fox News now considered middle-of-the-road, and more of the citizenry considering Alex Jones and Breitbart to be news sources, how much higher might that fringe portion of us grow to be? How many Jeffs are there out on the road, filled with conviction about what they believe to be true?

The problem is not that we have crazy people, or to be fair to the genuinely mentally ill, not that we have people who give crazy ideas a perch in their world view. The problem is that where once neighbors used to agree on who the crazy ones were, now we have groups of crazies genuinely convinced that the other side is crazy.

I guess I'm the other side. And yes, I have been called crazy by friends and family for my own beliefs and practices.

Back in 1978, when Joe and I made our way through Utah, a guy who spoke like 2018 Jeff would have been considered nuts. Now he has a following. He is a follower. He feels like part of his own conspiracy, and he has plenty of company.

That, and he is at the wheel of a very large truck.

# 16

## Itsy Bitsy Takes Me to The Golden Gate

In a town devoted to at least seven sins, I choose gluttony.

In a corner booth of a Wendover, Nevada, Burger King with a view of two casinos and the back door of a brothel, I watch the staff take their smoke breaks, munch on a Whopper and fries, and suck on a Coke from a plastic cup large enough to fill a canal from here to San Francisco. In violation of the sign by the soda fountain, I refill the monstrous jug with sugary, syrupy, bubbly brown water, and carry it back to my table.

Have you ever watched a street person at a gas station or a coffee shop pour industrial quantities of sugar into their coffee? Not knowing when you might next find a comfortable perch and a supply of food will do that to you. You'll take whatever is there, just because it's there. I am in very little danger of legitimate hunger, but something about heading back out into the desert makes me want to fill my gills, even at the risk of Type II diabetes.

Before I saddle up, a gray-haired retiree named Gary stops by my table. He has noticed my sign. Gary has the kind manner of a man grateful to be alive, which he very much is. He tells me all about his travels with his wife through Nebraska, Wyoming, the Dakotas, Louisiana, Arkansas. Now they are headed back to their home near Sacramento, for how long he does not know. "I've got some health issues," says Gary, which I sense is an understatement.

"We love Mother Nature's work," he says, with a smile indicating that he has clearly taken it all in. The Crazy Horse Memorial, which I have never seen, is his favorite. I'm a little puzzled by this. Chiseling the head of Custer's nemesis on that Dakota mountain was the work of a Polish guy with a lot of dynamite. Mother Nature probably winced and stuck both fingers in her ears.

Gary asks me to wait a minute. He goes out to the parking lot and vanishes into his RV. A few minutes later, I look up, and there he is again. Gary hands me a small stack of fast food coupons that he and his wife clipped from a magazine. They are held together neatly with a rubber band.

Thank you, Gary.

We shake hands and say goodbye. I sit there a moment, shaking my head in disbelief. While I was hiking through Craig, Colorado, a guy came running down the street, calling out to me, asking if I was hungry, if I wanted something to eat. "No one goes hungry around here," he hollered from half a block away.

I waved thanks and hollered back that I had just eaten. He persisted, "If you're hungry later, come back and we'll get you some food."

He could have just stayed in his house, but he saw a guy with a backpack walking by and that prompted him to call out, offering sustenance. I waved and shouted that I was fine, just looking for a ride. I never got his name.

There were ambivalent strangers, too, like the boy in Nebraska who tried to slip me dollar bills through his barely-open passenger window. He was scared, but he wasn't in the least bit scary. Instead, I dined on the kindness of Brodie and shared apple turnovers at the truck stop.

And now, Gary and his wife, coupon clippers from California, taking what seemed like their final trip of a lifetime, want to share their fast food bounty with me.

This is the country I'm supposed to fear?

These are the people I was told might kill me. Those people out there—strangers. So many strangers across this country want to make sure that I eat. Friends fed me, too. Sean. Karin. Deb.

Some, like Adam in Indiana, let me buy him food. But it is the memory of generous strangers like Gary and his wife that stick with me the most.

With my Whopper breakfast in my belly, I make my way back toward the highway once again. I am prepared to spend a long morning standing on the ramp. Roadside logic is barely logic at all, but it just seems fair that a good stretch on a ramp should be followed by a bad one. The last ride, with Jeff from Salt Lake, came along quickly. He was, at most, the tenth driver to see me there by the Denny's. I couldn't imagine being blessed twice in one day with such a short wait.

Wendover, Nevada, is dry and sunny, the air a perfectly pleasant temperature, and my water jug and my belly are full. Only seven hundred, thirty-five miles to San Francisco—maybe two days away?

A tall, disheveled guy is hitching the eastbound ramp. An enormous man, even against the backdrop of a vast desert sky, with an enormous head, he looks like a hungover Garrison Keillor, dressed in a well-worn tuxedo. But that pink-scalded skin—did he fall asleep in the sun? Maybe he has been working all night in a kitchen. Could it be that he just gambled till dawn and lost every cent he had, even the gas money?

I thought about Kelly from Wegman's, back in Canandaigua, and her hard-working tile- laying father who couldn't keep sober long enough to hang onto a driver's license. Maybe the man standing before me had so many DWIs that hitching was the only method of commuting left to him? I wonder how Kelly's dad is doing.

As I get closer, my mind runs wilder, and the giant man silhouetted against the blue sky looms larger and larger. Here's what I think happened. Garrison (I had already named him) worked all night, cashed his paycheck, lost a month's worth of earnings at the casino, then sold his car to place one last bet, which turned out to be a loser, and now he is forced to hitch home. That must be it.

If Jeff from Salt Lake can make up spacecraft shooting through cylindrical openings in the center of the Earth, I don't see any reason why I can't invent a life for the man standing on the side of the road in the ninety seconds or so I'm given to size him up. I am sure that drivers and passengers, shooting by me each day as I go from coast to coast, have been entertaining themselves by inventing dramas to fill in the blanks in my life story. Today, on a cool desert morning, two thousand miles from home, still four hundred barren miles from the Golden State, it's my turn to fantasize.

When I nod in greeting, Garrison shakes me off. He clearly does not want to share the ramp.

I walk past him, still wondering if he had spent the night earning his paycheck, losing it, or both. The presence of another hitching soul, even a grubby one, is a comforting sign that this might be a friendly town for a hitchhiker. The giant from A Prairie Home Companion seems relieved when I pass by him, walk under the overpass, turn left, and set up on the westbound ramp.

I am glad that I have not lost my white baseball cap. Utah's early morning sun was just getting started. I brace for a long day.

Twenty minutes after I set my pack down, a minivan stops. Will is going to Winnemucca. I have no idea where that is. I slide my pack into the back of the van, introduce myself to my driver and his co-pilot, an aging Toy Pomeranian named Itsy Bitsy. She looks like a stuffed doll.

Will has small blue eyes, a solid jaw, and a light pair of squared-off eyeglasses that seem a bit larger than necessary. Later on, when my friends see pictures of us, they note that, with our plaid shirts, gray hair, and glasses, Will and I could pass for family.

Itsy Bitsy clings to Will's lap, taking in this new arrival. The dog climbs down her master's leg and back up again, moves over to my seat for a sniff, then returns to Will's lap. She has some trust issues.

Winnemucca, I have since learned, is a town of about eight thousand souls and is home to the Pussy Cat Saloon and Brothel, as well as the C Horse Ranch. The C Horse is a great place to let your horse spend the night in between long days riding in a trailer across the desert. The Pussy Cat tends to the overnight needs of a different species. For my purposes, it is enough to hear that Winnemucca is two hundred miles closer to the Golden Gate.

Will has no plans to stay there. He is going to turn north there and head to Oregon, where he has some family ties.

The van is littered with wrappers from fast food operations— Wendy's, McDonald's, Burger King. A sturdy seventy-eight years old, Will does not discriminate in his choice of fatty foods and sugary drinks. He grips the wheel with both big strong hands and takes off.

The West has speed limits, though it might as well not. With so few cars on the road, and nothing but shoulder and desert on either side, what does it really matter how fast you go? We are just west of the Bonneville Salt Flats, where race drivers go to try to break the world land speed record.

Driving this desert with Will is like driving through the old neighborhood with one of my uncles. Uncle Dave was a school bus driver from the time when New York City neighborhoods were named by parish. He would drive you around and tell you the story of each street corner, where the church had been, when the first Korean grocer had moved in, when the old Italian guy who owned the deli got mugged, how there used to be a warehouse here, but now it's turned into a brew pub.

Will is like that, an encyclopedia of geography, except that his neighborhood is vast and populated with mines and metals. The Western Range from Utah to Oregon, Arizona to Idaho— this is his neighborhood. Will started digging precious stuff out of these hills and deserts when he was thirteen years old. There is not a stretch of this high desert that Will has not mined.

He waves a hand and shakes it toward the north. There was a tungsten vein over there, he tells me, copper a hundred miles south of the next turnoff, silver and cadmium around the next bend. He has a nose for metals, the way Bill Toneff, the centenarian back in Ohio, has a nose for birds.

"When I was thirteen, I set up a mine for a guy and made a hundred dollars," Will tells me. "At that time, my friends were making fifteen dollars a week. I said, I'm never going to work for another man again."

And, to hear him tell it, he has not. Will mined copper in Chile. He trucked gold over the Mexican border in a time when to do so was of questionable legality. He owns trucks that haul equipment and trucks that move ore, and trucks to move the heavy equipment he owns, machines with names I have never heard.

He is not physically imposing, but even before he tells me about the pistol and the rifle he carries in the van, something about him made clear that he could hold his own with anyone.

In the 1970s, Will joined the early rebels in what came to be called the Sagebrush Rebellion.

The Rebellion was a reaction among ranchers and miners to what they saw as the federal government telling them what they could and could not do with the land. Will saw himself less as a rebel and more as a homesteader, a guy who could fly his plane into the desert, dig a hole, and find something that he could turn into money. All he needs from government, as he sees it, is just to be left alone to dig these metals out of the earth.

The Sagebrush Rebellion flared up right around the time Joe and I had crossed the Western desert in the late seventies. Homesteading had ended, and the federal government held title to vast expanses of the West. People like Will resented the "Easterners," as he saw the feds, and they fought for local control of the Western rangelands, county by county.

Today, the question of federal land holdings is pretty much settled, though right-wing opportunists like the Bundy family occasionally stoke the flames. Will does not have a high opinion of environmentalists and he seems to hope that the current occupant of the White House will see things more his way. The word "Trump" only passes his lips once during the entire day we spend riding together.

Mostly, Will wants to talk about his wife, Doris. He calls her his queen. She was a devout Mormon, and though he never joined the church, Will put on a suit every Sunday and attended worship with her. She ran the house, and he made the money. Doris and Will were together forty years. It sounds like he took her to every cancer clinic he could find. He did all that he could, but she left him in February, just a few months ago.

Since Doris died, Will hasn't had a good night's sleep in his own home. At night, he crawls into a travel trailer that he keeps in the yard, closes his eyes, and rubs Itsy Bitsy's little head, hoping to doze off for a few hours. When that doesn't work, he packs up the dog, gets into the van, and drives. It doesn't matter much to him where he goes.

His cell phone rings. It is his brother in Idaho, a man he has not seen in fifteen years. "You and I got a lot of catching up to do," I hear Will say. Right then and there, they make a plan to get together on Will's way back from Oregon.

After he hangs up, he tells me about some property in Arizona he is selling to help out one of his granddaughters, and another house he's trying to get a family member to take over.

Everything about Will has the scent of someone trying to wrap things up, to fix things while he still has the tools.

His plan for today is to turn to the north at Winnemucca and drive all day until he reaches the place on the Oregon coast where his family started out. He hasn't been there in forever.

We pass a road sign: San Francisco 375 miles.

"I guess we can get you there by bedtime."

Did I hear that right?

"Will, that's way past Winnemucca."

Will's plan had been to turn north just another hundred miles into the desert, but instead he is offering to cut south through the Sierra Nevada mountains and take me all the way across California to the Bay Area. This means that before the day is done, he will be hundreds of miles away from his destination, and I will be at my niece's doorstep.

There is no disguising this monster-sized act of generosity, but Will, in a shy way, tries to minimize it. He likes the Bay Area, he tells me. He used to live there years ago (where had this man not laid his head?) and he is looking forward to a long drive up the coast. Will is happy to be out of the house in the Utah desert, eager to keep moving. I am a little concerned for Itsy Bitsy. That's a long day in the car.

We push westward. Desert turns to steppe and steppe fades into the pine forests of the Sierra.

Will hums along at an inhuman pace. When we stop to eat, I'm certain he will want to get out and stretch his legs. Not the case. He pulls into the drive-through window at a McDonald's, and we order two Big Macs plus some nuggets for Itsy Bitsy. I am tasked with feeding her the nuggets ounce by ounce over the next hour. Good appetite for such a little girl.

We come down out of the mountain.

California.

Is the Golden State my destination? Not really.

My plan has been to recreate the trip from 1978 as much as possible, which had taken us to a lot of places, including the Grand Canyon and New Orleans. I had told friends that I had only three weeks to spare before work and family obligations would force me back home.

But manifest destiny manifested itself mightily. As I traveled this time, everyone back home begins to cheer me on as if I were racing to get to the coast.

Which in some sense I suppose I am. But mostly I'm just on the road, seeing where it takes me, poking around to see if this place we call the road is still alive.

If Will has anything to say about it, the road is still out there, alive and welcoming, and about as safe a place as anywhere you'd want to be—especially if, as I've been reminded time and time again, you're white like me. I think of all the times I've heard people talk about the crazy people who will pick me up and the dangerous situations I will find myself in, and here I am, riding in a Caravan with a grandpa in the driver's seat and a Toy Pomeranian sleeping on my lap.

The ribbon of lights of the Bay Bridge dazzles me. Am I the same person who was stranded and frustrated by the Jug 'N Loaf in Craig, Colorado, just two days back? Is this the same city that Joe and I visited forty years ago?

I'm still the same guy, in an older version. San Francisco has been altered by more than age. AIDS, Harvey Milk, the World Series earthquake, Facebook, the TPP—that was all still to be written when Joe and I crossed the Golden Gate in August 1978, in the back of a pickup truck headed for Sausalito.

The kindness that got us there—that is a constant.

Will is determined to deliver me directly to family, in the person of my niece Tara and her husband, Jesse. Thanks to the smartphone and GPS, which only existed in research labs forty years ago, we pull off the highway within six blocks of their apartment. Tara, recently graduated from law school, six months pregnant, and studying for the bar exam, hops out of her Prius and greets both me and Will like long-lost family.

She embraces Will and pets Itsy Bitsy. We invite Will to join us for a cup of tea or a sandwich, but he wants to keep moving. He smiles happily to see a young couple starting their lives. I ask where he is going to sleep.

He says he'll just keep driving up the coast until he feels like stopping. Will and his wife had spent some time together in the Bay Area years back, and he wants to soak in the memories that are coming back to him.

I understand.

In the parking lot under the bridge we say our goodbyes.

Will and Itsy Bitsy get back on the road.

# Epilogue:
# Earbuds and Tinted Windows

The Road doesn't end there. It follows me home. After three lovely days in San Francisco, I fly back to Syracuse. In just five hours, I trace my way back over the country I had crossed in eighteen days, with just a hashtag, sign, and a backpack.

Somewhere down below the clouds, Will and Itsy Bitsy are making their way back to Utah. I hope he gets to see his brother. Jeff might still be cruising the desert listening to Alex Jones or searching for furniture. Nazz made it back and finished her last day of school; she sent me an email saying that her stomachache had vanished as quickly as it came on.

Steam still seeps from the bubbling mountain streams at Steamboat Springs and Strawberry Park.

Danica is getting back to work in the forest. Chris is slinging bacon broccoli slaw at Johnny B Good's. In Craig, Colorado, Richard is probably loading his little dog, Casey, in the car and getting ready to drive another patient to the doctor. Brodie is serving defrosted turnovers at the Love's Truck Stop in Nebraska, and Scott's family is no doubt talking basketball over breakfast.

"I Go By Johnny" could be almost anywhere, but if I had to guess, I'd say he's sleeping off a drunken binge behind the McDonald's in Omaha.

I picture James, my favorite mason, with two fingers on the wheel of his pickup, sipping coffee with the other hand, while rolling down the road in Lexington, Kentucky, him and TJ on their way to meet Chicken at work. Back in Ohio, Bill Toneff, nearing his 100th birthday, would be waking to see what new birds will brighten his dawn.

Ricardo? God only knows. Hopefully, he's still on this side of prison's gates.

I wonder when Morgan, Harmony's mom, will be hearing back

from the Children's Hospital in Pittsburgh. I smile thinking of badass Portia finishing a late shift at Denny's and worry for John and Carl still trying to scratch a living from beaten-down stretches of the Rust Belt. I say a quiet prayer for Mike's mom in Willoughby Heights, and for the baby about to be born to the woman addicted to meth, whom I saw lying on the floor in the Peoria bus station. What will this life offer to that child?

People who had taken a chance on me, as I had on them, and whose stories had become important to me, are going on with their lives.

Now, I'm in the middle seat of three. On the window sits Angel, who lives in Oakland, but is flying back today to Medellin, Colombia, returning home for the first time in years. He's barely thirty years old. Angel grew up in Medellin when his hometown was the center of the hemisphere's cocaine trade.

He lived through that violence and escaped to the Bay Area, where street life caught up to him. Angel gets around in a wheelchair now, a bullet in his spine, and he spends his days in Oakland city schools, trying to show other young people a different way to live.

He says it's time to go home. That's a trip that might worry even me, but he has the aura of a man at peace. Times have changed, says Angel. Like dozens of people I met on the road, he had a story he needed to tell.

It seems like everyone who stopped for me wanted to be heard. On the road, people open up more than just their car doors. They share stories sometimes because of joys or pains we have in common, sometimes because they're angry, and other times for no apparent reason, just because there is someone to listen.

Mike's dying mother, Kelly's drunk dad. Steve-the-surveyor's love of sailboats, retired Steve's closeted dreams of taking off with his wife to chance one last cross-country spree.

Stories.

Yeah, I think the road is still out there.

Up close, it feels like we are an entire nation driving the highways in search of someone to listen to us. From a distance, we appear more divided and scared than we really are. Some media anchors make sport of dividing the country into blue and red maps that assume if you know what someone thinks about a given issue, you can say with confidence what they will think of a hundred others. There is a value to categories, but I put greater stock in stories.

The road is a place inside us, where our yearnings meet our doubts, and we make a choice to find out what each day has to offer. Some days we choose to keep driving by. Some days we stop and listen.

I took a chance, and I'm grateful to the dozens of men and women who took a chance on me. It didn't seem risky to most of them. It was just the thing to do, something they each needed to do, maybe like I did, to find out if we are all still in this together.

We are all out on the road sometime.

But the way we take to the road has changed in forty years. Tinted windows. I can't see your face when you drive by. Earbuds. I can't hear the person next to me, don't know what music she likes. Gated communities. Realtors say half of people shopping for homes worry and place security at the top of their wish list.

The disappearance of hitchhiking and the rise of the gated community seem part of the same thing. Fear leads to isolation leads to more fear. Behind the walls we build, and the tinted glass, and the earbuds, we still search for community.

That fierce need to tell our story is the driver behind the biggest change in our lifetimes, the rise of the virtual world. The explosion of social media proves how badly we want connection.

Online, we get to control the settings.

Not so on the road. Hitchhiking is a surrender of control. It's a radical proposition both for the driver and the one with the thumb out. Stop the car, open that door, and you open yourself up in a radical way. You talk, and you listen. For ten minutes or hundreds of miles.

Based on my trip, I am tempted to believe that we can still lay claim to being one people, if we can only figure out how to really listen.

I wanted to believe that we can still make it from coast to coast together. I found that there still is a "we," but with one large, classically American exception.

I had been home for a month when I ran into my friend Mark at a community meeting. Mark is on the city school board. He is also a college professor, youth counselor, and the local leader of the Nation of Islam. Mark was excited to catch up. He had heard about the trip. "I'm not sure I could do what you did," he said.

It was meant as a compliment of sorts, but I blurted out my honest reaction: "You should not."

My mind went to a different place, to a bar of happy Klansmen getting ready to party; to the ranting Uber driver, Melvin, in Peoria; and the worried look on Dave's face when he told me about the deaf black man he had met less than fifty miles from here.

This land may have been made for you and me, but it is, at this historical moment, a lot more hospitable for people who look like me, than for people who look like Mark.

On the road in 1978, I felt like part of something. The '60s and '70s had been a humbling time. We as a people had been reminded again of our failings, and as Joe and I crisscrossed the country that summer, we had a sense of a people trying to be better. We knew that we could do a lot better by one another. At least, we felt we should give it a good try.

When Joe and I got a ride with a Mississippi farmer who used the N word, just like any other word in normal conversation, it was not a stretch to think of him as a member of a dying breed. Today, I'm not so sure.

On this trip, I saw frightening evidence of empowered and emboldened racism. A chunk of the white population, and I can't know how large a chunk that is, feels like they have had enough. They don't need to use the N word. They've got their own tribe, their own grievances, their flag, and a leader in the most powerful office in the land, one they believe has got their back.

In 1978, Joe and I saw a good number of African American hitchhikers. We were picked up by black drivers, shared rides and the road with quite a few. It was normal. But not this time. Only one black man, a veteran amputee who chose not to share his name, and no black woman shared the roadside. No black drivers picked me up.

Two drivers made overt racist comments, and two drivers mentioned with a certain sadness that they didn't think I would have any luck hitching in their neck of the woods if I weren't white. Through fifteen states, I didn't share the road with a single black driver.

That should not surprise, given the noise coming out of the White House and the resurgence of white nationalism worldwide. But it does sadden. Not that we were reaching the Promised Land in 1978, but it seemed that, back then, we at least had to try. Now it seems like a lot of us have given up. And a good number of white people seem fed up with all this talk of equality.

Not long after I got home, I gave a ride to Suzanne, a tall woman in her forties, with stringy blond hair and stitches in the front of her mouth, where once there were teeth. She was walking toward downtown Syracuse with her thumb out. Suzanne had come here a few weeks back, following a man, a bad man, it turns out, and from what I could gather in our few minutes together, not the first one to come into her life.

Suzanne's dad had warned her about this guy before she left Phoenix. She was too ashamed to call home to ask for money. "Just take me to the highway, so I can fly a sign," she requested, showing me the scribbled cardboard sign. She needed exactly one hundred and eighty-four dollars to get a bus ticket back to Arizona. She knew her trade. With confidence, she predicted that she'd have begged enough by the time the sun went down to get her on the 2:00 AM bus, heading west.

A few weeks later, I was driving Route 20 between Otisco Lake and Syracuse, when a young man with a bushy red beard popped out of a cornfield and set himself up on the side of the road. His name was Ryan and he was from South Dakota. He had been making his way across the country for a month.

He could have been the 1978 version of me. I took him to McDonald's for breakfast, gave him five dollars, and left him by the interstate. He was planning to hitch to Albany and kayak south to New York City. I warned him that the Hudson River currents were not friendly or safe for amateur kayakers. Big-eyed Ryan wandering Times Square—that would be a sight to see.

Months after returning home, my last ride, Will, and I find one another on Facebook. He sent me some sad news. Itsy Bitsy had passed away two months after our trip. The vet said she was "grieving for the wife." I'll bet she was. Just like Will.

We began to follow one another on Facebook, and the man I see on my little screen doesn't seem like the man I spent time with, the kind, grumpy Grandpa, petting his Toy Pomeranian and giving a lift to hitchhikers.

Facebook Will posts things other people have compiled, and he doesn't seem to get a lot of attention. He thinks mosques should be shut down and Muslims banned from Congress. He'd like to see Donald Trump re-elected and followed in the White House by his namesake son. I don't know how deep these ideas rest in him. Could be just his rebellious side.

Or it could be a whole lot worse.

I'm gonna keep hitching, keep trying to find out. If you see me, stop if you can. If not, I'll try to wave. Maybe you'll be out there on the road one day. I'll try to remember what it's like and remember to stop.

# Acknowledgements

My utmost gratitude goes out to those who shared a piece of the road, whether they picked me up, offered advice, shared pastry, lodging, and laughter. You each gave me a great gift— something to write about.

Thanks to my agent, Tara Gonsowski, and to my editors, Jim McKeever, Jean Albanese, Richard Marsh, and Rickey Gard Diamond. To Michelle Breidenbach and Willson Cummer for offering moral support and the ingenious wristbands. Gary Weinstein and William Sunderlin helped underwrite my travel expenses, and Tim Bryant took care of my massage practice while I was on the road. Thanks to Sean Kirst for inspiration, lodging, and for writing the foreword; and to Joe Campo, for making that first trip with me in 1978, and recording the audio version of this book.

My every journey begins and ends in the same place, with Ellen Haffar, who loves me enough to say goodbye, and then hello, and is also responsible for the artwork that introduces each chapter. Thanks, dear one, for traveling this road with me.

I hope to see you all on the road soon.

Ellen Haffar

**Ed Griffin-Nolan** wanders, runs, sails, and writes. In 1978 he hitchhiked across the US, and forty years later he repeated the feat, chronicling his adventures across a vastly changed nation.

In between those two journeys, he worked as a journalist in his hometown of Syracuse, NY, and written from Latin America and the Middle East. He has lived in Pinochet's Chile, Sandinista Nicaragua, and traveled to Iraq in the aftermath of Desert Storm. His works have appeared in the LA Times, Chicago Tribune, Miami Herald, the Nation magazine, and the Syracuse New Times. The father of three grown children, he lives in Pompey, New York with his wife, Ellen, an artist, and their gregarious Labradoodle, Gracie. His day job is massage therapy.

## Also Available from Rootstock Publishing:

*The Atomic Bomb on My Back*
Taniguchi Sumiteru

*Blue Desert*
Celia Jeffries

*China in Another Time: A Personal Story*
Claire Malcolm Lintilhac

*Fly with A Murder of Crows: A Memoir*
Tuvia Feldman

*Junkyard at No Town*
J.C. Myers

*The Language of Liberty:*
*A Citizen's Vocabulary*
Edwin C. Hagenstein

*The Lost Grip: Poems*
Eva Zimet

*Lucy Dancer*
Story and Illustrations by Eva Zimet

*Nobody Hitchhikes Anymore*
Ed Griffin-Nolan

*Preaching Happiness: Creating a Just*
*and Joyful World*
Ginny Sassaman

*Red Scare in the Green Mountains:*
*Vermont in the McCarthy Era 1946-1960*
Rick Winston

*Safe as Lightning: Poems*
Scudder H. Parker

*Street of Storytellers*
Doug Wilhelm

*Tales of Bialystok: A Jewish Journey*
*from Czarist Russia to America*
Charles Zachariah Goldberg

*To the Man in the Red Suit: Poems*
Christina Fulton

*Uncivil Liberties: A Novel*
Bernie Lambek

*The Violin Family*
Melissa Perley; Illustrated by
Fiona Lee Maclean

*Wave of the Day: Collected Poems*
Mary Elizabeth Winn

*Whole Worlds Could Pass Away:*
*Collected Stories*
Rickey Gard Diamond